OP 17

Out of Bounds

Transnational Sanctuary in Irregular Warfare

by
Thomas A. Bruscino, Jr.

Combat Studies Institute Press
Fort Leavenworth, Kansas

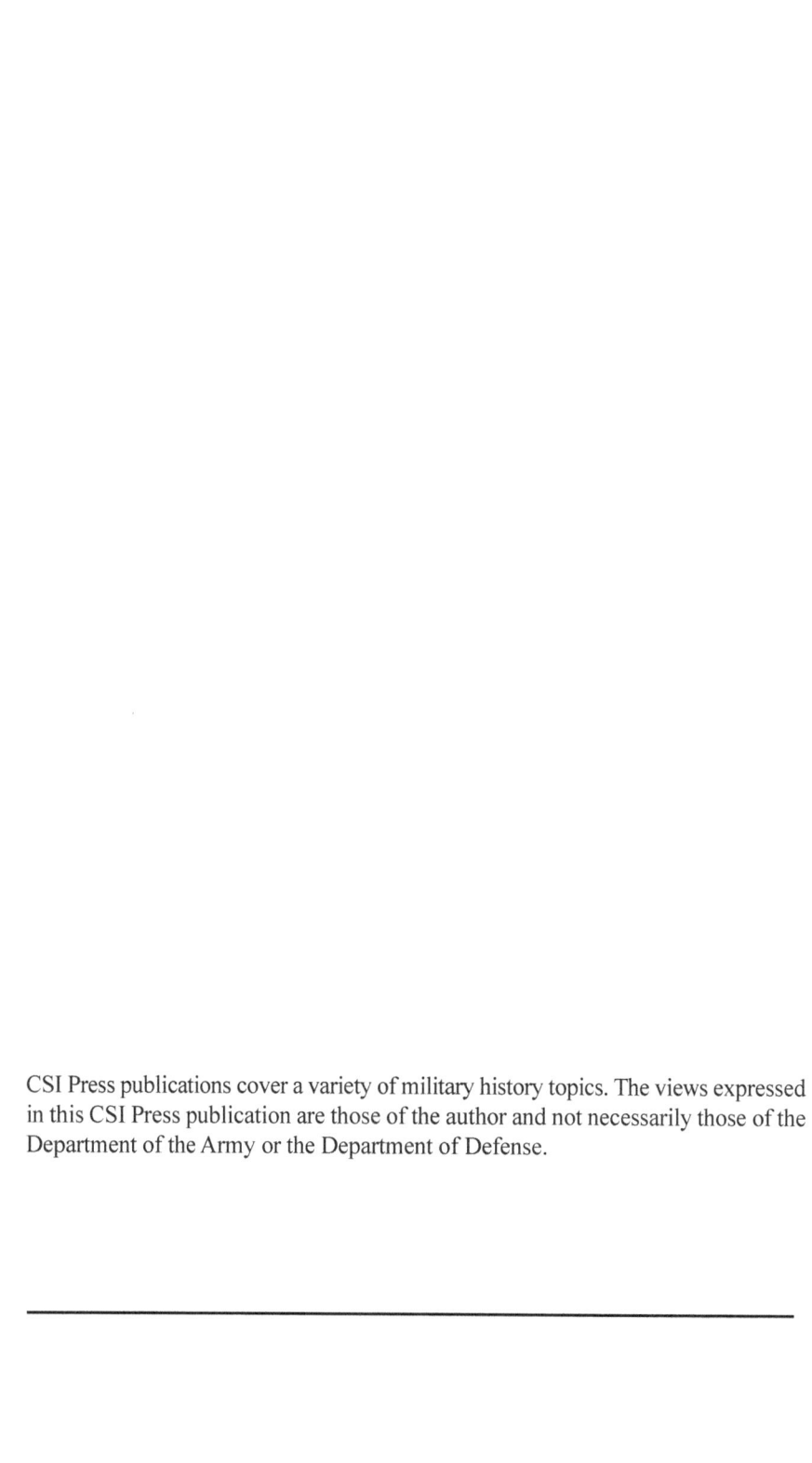

Foreword

In this timely Occasional Paper, Dr. Tom Bruscino analyzes a critical issue in the GWOT, and one which has bedeviled counterinsurgents past and present. He examines the role played by sanctuaries as they relate to irregular warfare in two conflicts. An active sanctuary refers to the practice of using territory outside the geographical limits of an irregular war to provide various forms of support to one side, usually the insurgent or guerrilla force.

In the first case study, he looks at the United States' efforts to defeat the advantages gained by the Viet Cong (and later the North Vietnamese Army) by the use of sanctuaries in Cambodia and Laos during the Vietnam War. In doing so, he points out the diplomatic, military, and economic challenges which develop when trying to prevent the use of transnational sanctuaries by irregular forces. In the second case study, he examines the Soviet incursion into Afghanistan in the 1980s, but this time he does so from the perspective of the insurgency, the Mujahideen. Bruscino illustrates the advantages accrued by the Afghan resistance in the use of Pakistan as a sanctuary; the Soviet efforts to neutralize those advantages; and the Mujahideen's responses to overcome the Soviet actions.

In both cases the author finds that the use of an active sanctuary by the insurgents was a major component of their eventual victory. Without a sanctuary it is hard to see how the Viet Cong/NVA or the Mujahideen could have succeeded. In regards to a sanctuary, it is hard to see how the U.S./South Vietnamese or the Soviet Union could have defeated the insurgencies. Active sanctuaries present the counterinsurgent with a host of military problems, but denying an insurgent the use of an active sanctuary is far more than a military task. All the elements of national power must be employed if one hopes to defeat the challenge posed by active sanctuaries.

We at the Combat Studies Institute hope that the insights presented in this monograph will be of great value to military planners in the current war against terrorism. *CSI – The Past is Prologue!*

Timothy R. Reese
COL, AR
Director, Combat Studies Institute

Acknowledgements

An author incurs many debts in the course of writing any project of this sort, and I am no different. The entire staff of the Combat Studies Institute and the Combined Arms Research Library at Fort Leavenworth have been nothing but supportive throughout the process, but a few individuals deserve special mention. I am indebted to Bob Ramsey for kindly passing on a wealth of material that got me started; John McGrath and Matt Matthews for their thoughtful commentary; and Dr. William G. Robertson for sharing an unpublished paper on the topic of sanctuaries that helped provide focus to this study.

The supervisory team and editorial board of Colonel Timothy R. Reese, Director Combat Studies Institute; Dr. Robertson, Deputy Director, CSI and CAC Command Historian; Lieutenant Colonel (Retired) Steven E. Clay, Chief, Research and Publications Team; and Major (Retired) Kendall D. Gott, Supervisory Historian, Research and Publications Team, all helped usher this paper along with sage advice and needed corrections.

On the production side, it was my great good luck to have Robin Kern to make the maps; she did a wonderful job. Likewise, two Combat Studies Institute editors, Angela Bowman and Mike Brooks, did remarkable work in clarifying my muddled thoughts, tightening my writing, preparing the manuscript for publication, and generally saving me from countless mistakes. I cannot thank them, and everyone else who helped on this project, enough. Of course, any mistakes herein are mine and mine alone.

Lastly, my wife Terrie and my sons Dominic and Anthony endured a cross-country move so that I could come to the Combat Studies Institute to work on this project. Their sacrifices made all of this possible, and I could not do it without them.

Contents

Foreword iii

Acknowledgements v

List of Maps ix

Introduction...1

    Borders in the War 1

    Sanctuaries and Modern History 6

    American Traditions 8

    Two Case Studies..9

Chapter 1. Vietnam...15

    Indications 15

    The Dimensions of the Problem 18

    First Options 21

    Airpower...25

    Pacification and Ground Incursions...............................30

    Ending the War 36

Chapter 2. Soviet–Afghan War...49

    Shock 49

    Background..50

    The Resistances and Their Friends 52

    The Borders 55

    Early Fighting, Early Adjustments 58

    Those Missiles 64

    Soviet Wtihdrawal, Afghanistan's Half Victory 67

Conclusion 79

    Vietnam and Afghanistan Compared.............................79

    Sanctuary Doctrine 80

    The Contemporary Picture...82

    What Can Be Done? 85

Bibliography 91

About the Author..109

List of Maps

1. Vietnam and the Ho Chi Minh Trail Network 17

2. The 1970 Cambodia Incursions 33

3. Santuaries on the Afghanistan / Pakistan Border.................................... 51

4. Parrot's Beak Region on Afghanistan / Pakistan Border 63

Introduction

Borders in the War

The very name the United States has given to its struggle against fundamentalist Muslim terrorists indicates that international borders do not confine the enemy. "The Global War on Terrorism" is just that, a war waged around the globe on a foe bound not by the strands of state or nation, but by a perverted and perverse ideology. Nevertheless, because the United States and its allies share a respect for the international system, they have chosen to fight this enemy primarily within the boundaries of two states: Afghanistan and Iraq.

Despite their adherence to ideology, the terrorists understand and use the international system; despite their dismissal of nations and states for their version of one united pure religion, they gladly hide behind the veil of state boundaries. Some states oppose the terrorists but are incapable of completely stopping this use of their territories. Others—for reasons ranging from regional power politics, to sympathy for terrorist ideology, to hostility to the United States and its allies—either directly support the terrorists, or knowingly allow then to make use of their lands. Therefore, international borders, and the transnational sanctuaries and supply lines that they protect, have become a crucial issue in the global war on terrorism. Counterinsurgent forces ignore or downplay the problem at their own peril.

Transnational sanctuaries have played a role in the war on terrorism from the onset of the first campaigns. Shortly after the Americans and their allies took Kabul in the fall of 2001, the Taliban and al-Qaeda terrorists retreated to the mountainous Afghan frontier with Pakistan. In the Tora Bora region south of Jalalabad, they made use of old supply stores to dig into the mountains and valleys and continue the fight. In December, allied forces launched a series of assaults on the enemy positions, eventually killing and capturing many of the terrorists. However, some escaped across the border into Pakistan, including perhaps, Osama bin Laden himself. In the March 2002 Operation ANACONDA near the Pakistan border south of Kabul, events followed a similar course. Coalition troops encircled al-Qaeda positions in a mountain valley roughly 25 miles from the border. The terrorists stood and fought before collapsing and breaking into smaller groups to flee to Pakistan.[1]

Since the spring of 2002, the terrorist forces in Afghanistan have yet to reconstitute into large enough forces to stand and fight. They have, however, attempted to launch an insurgency from the borderlands with Pakistan. The government of Pakistan is a Coalition ally in the war on terror, but has only partial control of the tribal areas along the country's border with Afghanistan. Intelligence has indicated that many of the leaders of al-Qaeda have found refuge in these regions, and the terrorists have had some success in launching limited attacks in Afghanistan and returning to the border. In response, the border region has been one of the key areas of focus for Coalition forces over the last few years, but not without controversy.

Pakistani officials have repeatedly asserted that their "forces are fully capable of securing and protecting Pakistan's borders."[2] Indeed Pakistani forces have worked, sometimes alongside American intelligence, to kill and arrest hundreds of al-Qaeda in Pakistan.[3] In the meantime Coalition forces have periodically launched raids or air strikes along, and sometimes over, the border in search of the terrorists and their leaders.[4] The most prominent of the recent efforts came in January 2006, when a US airstrike targeting al-Qaeda leaders in the border village of Damadola may have killed civilians in the village, resulting in civilian protests against Pakistan's government for cooperating with the United States.[5] Afterward, Afghan president Hamid Karzai and Pakistani president Pervez Musharraf had a brief public dispute over Pakistani efforts to police the borders.[6] The tenuous situation along the frontier continues to this day.

Iraq's borders and neighbors are even more problematic. The planners of the war had the simultaneous (and somewhat contradictory) objectives of isolating Iraq from its neighbors while influencing change within those neighboring countries.[7] The neighbor concerning planners the most was Syria, and part of the invasion plan sent American units to western Iraq to block the Syrian border. Turkey's refusal to allow Coalition forces to use Turkish territory as a staging point for the attack hindered these plans and forced the Coalition to use an effective, but necessarily less thorough, combination of special forces, conventional forces, and Kurdish allies in western and northwestern Iraq during the March 2003 invasion.[8]

Reports indicated that before the March attacks, Saddam Hussein began bringing in foreign nationals from Syria to fight the Coalition.[9] The border remained open in the early stages of the fighting and even Saddam's sons briefly fled to Syria.[10] During the open combat operations, US Central Command commander General Tommy Franks received reports of "civilian bus convoys full of foreign fighters... coming in from Syria. Arabs from all over. Maybe even some Chechens. They are bad actors, but it's gonna be tough to target them while their riding on civilian buses."[11] Coalition forces found themselves engaged with foreign fighters early and often in the fighting.[12] Franks became so frustrated with Syria's apparent complicity with the growing insurgency that he ordered the shutdown of Iraqi oil pipelines to Syria.[13] In April 2003 Deputy Defense Secretary Paul Wolfowitz told the Senate Armed Services Committee, "In recent days the Syrians have been shipping killers into Iraq to try to kill Americans.... If they continue, then we need to think about what our policy is with respect to a country that harbors terrorists...." Wolfowitz did not call for direct action against Syria, maintaining instead that "by calling attention to it we hope that in fact that may be enough to get them to stop."[14]

The Syrian border continued to be a problem after the end of major conventional operations in May 2003. L. Paul Bremer, the Administrator of the Coalition Provisional Authority in Iraq, wrote in his memoirs of a July 2003 discussion of the major problems in Iraq:

> Since the collapse of Saddam in April, Iraq's long, porous border with Syria had offered the primary escape route for fleeing Baathists and Islamic extremist fighters' main infiltration vector into Iraq.... The United States had publicly leaned on Syria to suppress this activity. But Syria, ruled by its own Baathist Party, seemed immune to most diplomatic or economic leverage and might only be susceptible to direct military intervention. President Bashar Assad, son of Syria's late dictator Hafiz Assad, knew this was unlikely with US forces engaged in Iraq and Afghanistan.[15]

As a result, insurgents continued to enter Iraq from Syria.

By the fall of 2003 the United States responded by stepping up its efforts against the Syrians. The American House of Representatives passed a resolution allowing sanctions against Syria, and the military took a more active role on the border.[16] The 101st Airborne Division was responsible for operations in northwestern Iraq—operations that included border security on a roughly 170-mile section of the border with Syria. One of the brigade commanders of the 101st noted:

> ...for the missions we had, I thought we had enough soldiers to do the job with the possible exception of controlling/patrolling the Syrian Border.... The border was difficult even for our small area, and it was especially difficult under conditions of limited visibility, given the rampant smuggling, and few bor-

3

der posts. Once we established an Iraqi Border Security force, border security improved greatly due to revamping Iraqi border forts, and equipping Iraqis with vehicles, weapons, training, and the wherewithal to do this important mission.[17]

Unfortunately, when the 101st left in February 2004, the Iraqi security forces performed poorly and border security lagged once again.[18]

The 3d Armored Cavalry Regiment (ACR) ran similar operations in Al Anbar Province in western Iraq—which shared an approximate 185-mile border with Syria. The regimental commander noted that one of their main problems was infiltration from the area around Al Qaim, where the Euphrates River enters Iraq from Syria:

> This was a troublesome area, particularly the area up by Rawa. This is a real rat line of people that would come in from Syria, up along Rawa, and down to Haditha. At Haditha they can either go down to Ramadi, in past Fallujah, and into Baghdad or they can move north to Baiji and then up to Mosul in the north. So this is a strategic rat line.[19]

The 3d ACR also increased the tempo of operations on the border in the fall of 2003. In Operation RIFLES BLITZ, the regiment worked with a battalion from the 101st to clear the border towns of Al Qaim and shut down all traffic to and from Syria for 10 days. They captured more than 300 prisoners, and at one point stopped a car at a checkpoint that held two Saudis and a Yemeni. The regimental commander recalled, "They had a journal with them and they were Jihadist. The journal put out a lot of contacts throughout the country. Of course, we turned this over to some other agencies so they could exploit it. But it was really the first physical proof that there were foreign fighters and they were being networked through Iraq."[20]

In order to affect better security along the frontier, the regiment broke down the border into sectors and set up schedules to observe various areas of infiltration. Air Force and Navy pilots flew observation missions, as did unmanned aerial vehicles. They also buried seismic sensors called steel rattlers to detect moving vehicles at the border. But the regiment had to cover a huge section of territory and never completely shut down the border. Part of the problem was the ingenuity of the insurgents. One officer recalled:

> ...foreign fighters come in a lot of different ways. We stopped water trucks that had false tanks with guys in them. So, that

4

is one of the things as far as a border crossing, there is a lot of commercial traffic. You might have a truck that is loaded with fruit, but they could have a false hiding place where there are rocket propelled grenades (RPGs) and weapons and stuff stacked up, and you just don't have the time to unload a complete truck and then load it back up.[21]

Over the past two years, infiltrations and operations have continued all along the Syrian frontier. All the while, the United States has pressured Syria to control its border, and Coalition and Iraqi forces have struggled to prevent the infiltration of foreign fighters and outside weaponry.[22]

The long Iraqi border with Iran also remains a concern. Planners assumed that the threat of a sizable Coalition force in the region combined with Iran's traditional animosity toward Saddam Hussein's Iraq would mean that the Iranians would stay out of the fight.[23] In the early part of the campaign it appeared that this assumption was correct. However, as early as May 2003, reports filtered in that a group of Iranian radicals had made its way into Iraq with the intent of influencing the post-Saddam government.[24] Coalition leaders noted that Iranian foreign fighters in Iraq seemed to increase over the next year.[25] In the spring of 2004, the Coalition took active steps to police the border, including closing down 16 of 19 open border crossings, funding 8,000 more border guards, and setting up a computerized passport system. Despite these efforts, Bremer conceded that "We are never going to have 100% security on the borders of Iraq—we have to be realistic about that."[26]

Indeed by the fall of 2005, reports indicated that the increased deadliness of insurgent improvised explosive devices came in part from new supplies of Iranian TNT, which one guerrilla called "about seven times stronger than the TNT available in Iraq."[27] In March 2006, US General John Abazaid confirmed such reports, telling the Senate Armed Services Committee that the insurgents had started using Iranian IED components and that "terrorists in northeastern Iraq used the Iranian northwestern border to move back and forth across the border."[28]

The exact extent of the foreign fighter components of the insurgencies in Afghanistan and Iraq are unclear, as are the precise numbers of weapons, ammunition, and supplies coming across international borders to aid the insurgents in the two countries. However, what is clear is that foreign nationals have from the beginning fought against the Americans and their allies in both Afghanistan and Iraq. And just as clear is the fact that both insurgencies have received outside aid from across international borders.

The United States and its allies have a problem with transnational sanctuary and supply lines in the global war on terrorism.

Sanctuaries and Modern History

Insurgencies are not a contemporary phenomenon. Throughout human history, smaller, less well-equipped groups have engaged in guerrilla-style warfare against larger powers. Even parts of the American War of Independence, especially in the southern colonies, took on the form of insurgent warfare. But insurgencies certainly became more prevalent in the 20th century, often as part of attempts to expel western powers from their colonial empires. After 1945, local insurgencies frequently became battlegrounds in the Cold War international rivalry between the United States and the Soviet Union.

Western powers were key players in the creation of the modern system of nation-states, and as a result tended to respect that system of international boundaries. Military violations of the wrong borders could mean all-out conventional war—with ghastly results—including the world wars of the 20th century. The proliferation of nuclear weapons after World War II meant that any all-out war among nuclear powers could be catastrophic. It was only a matter of time before insurgents would come to realize that they could take advantage of such a system.

The Cold War provided opportunity. In the years after World War II, the great powers took advantage of every chance to aid the enemies of their enemies. For the United States and its allies that most often meant support for pro-Western and anticommunist governments as they fought off communist-supported insurgencies. Conversely, the Soviet Union, and later China, helped trigger many of these contests by giving incentive, aid, and advice to communist, procommunist, or just anti-Western insurgencies— wherever they might emerge. The aid had to get to rebels somehow, and in those countries that were not islands, that meant turning to contiguous territories.

It is a short jump from using a contiguous country for supply lines to developing those lines into full-scale logistic, training, and launching bases. Insurgency expert Bernard Fall called such areas "active sanctuary," which he defined as "a territory contiguous to a rebellious area which, though ostensibly not involved in the conflict, provides the rebel side with shelter, training facilities, equipment, and—if it can get away with it—troops."[29] The threat of larger war and the feigned neutrality of the countries housing the active sanctuaries for the most part kept the rebels safe across the border.[30] A key aspect of a successful insurgency had been born.

Rebels quickly put active sanctuary to use throughout the world. In the Greek Civil War (1946-1949), the communist rebels enjoyed the use of sanctuaries in Albania, Yugoslavia, and Bulgaria. The communist insurgents fighting the British-supported government in Malaya from 1948 to 1960 had some sanctuaries in neighboring Thailand. Anti-French rebels in Indochina (1946-1954) could look to China for supply and refuge, and anti-French fighters in the Algerian War of Independence (1954-1962) had sanctuaries in Morocco and Tunisia. In all of these cases, the insurgents were generally successful as long as they had access to, and made use of, their sanctuaries.

Anti-rebel forces scrambled to find a response to this dilemma. In every case, circumstances mitigated against the natural inclination to invade in force and take out the sanctuaries, so other options had to be explored. The Greeks never did manage to close down their frontiers, but Yugoslavian leader Josef Tito sealed his own border due to divisions within the communist bloc. Under pressure within Greece and without outside support, the communist insurgency fell apart. In Malaya the rebels never took full advantage of the territory in Thailand and the Thai government grew generally hostile toward their efforts anyway. That insurgency became isolated in enclaves along the border and never gained any traction after 1960.[31]

The French struggled enough with the communist Vietminh rebels within Indochina and never made any headway in sealing the border with China. They lost their former colony in 1954. Algerian rebels used the borders with impunity in the early years of their fight, but the French had learned their lesson from Indochina. They built an extensive barrier system called the Morice Line stretching some 200 miles from the Mediterranean Sea to the Sahara Desert. The line consisted of an eight-foot electric fence surrounded by minefields and barbed wire. Roughly 80,000 French soldiers patrolled the barrier, and sensors along the fence indicated when and where insurgents tried to breach the line so that the French troops could quickly respond. According to one estimate, the fence proved so effective that it cut infiltration by 90 percent. Though the insurgency struggled militarily after that, other political issues forced the French to withdraw.[32]

In these cases of insurgencies, and many more, the existence of active sanctuaries did not guarantee victory for insurgencies, and nor did the lack of them guarantee defeat. But those insurgencies having access to active sanctuaries and outside support generally fared better than those that did not. And, as the United States was about to learn, such even held true when superpowers became involved in counterinsurgencies.

American Traditions

Even in the busy years for revolutionaries immediately after World War II, the American military focused on a large war with the Soviet Union and did little to develop its counterinsurgency doctrine. The dearth of American doctrine on irregular warfare did not mean that the United States had not engaged in a wide variety of low intensity conflicts. On the contrary, by the 1960s Americans had fought dozens of small wars, ranging from the fights with American Indians to any number of expeditions to Latin America and various islands in the Pacific in the decades around the turn of the 20th century. As recently as the 1940s, the United States had played a major role in defeating the Hukbalahap Insurrection in the Philippines.

Yet none of these campaigns led to a well-developed, written American doctrine for counterinsurgency—with the notable exception of the 1935 Marine Corps Small Wars Manual that was overshadowed by World War II and the looming conflict with the Soviets. Nevertheless, these low intensity conflicts did create inherited institutional tendencies for dealing with irregular warfare. Generally, American military thinkers looked at guerrilla warfare with disdain, and at guerrillas as brigands who reduced the art of war to a base crime and should be punished accordingly. When it came to the issue of sanctuary, the most important American tendency was to pursue those brigands to their villages, hideouts, and other bases of supply, and destroy them there. Beyond that, the American military put little thought into the problem.[33]

Then came the Vietnam War.

Two Case Studies

Despite a mighty effort in that war, one of the world's great superpowers proved unable to help a fledgling nation preserve its existence in the face of a relentless enemy. Vietnam became an ugly scar on the American psyche, a symbol of a military disaster never to be repeated. Not wanting to revisit the disaster, the military has for too long ignored many of the most important lessons of the war. Robert Cassidy explains this shortcoming: "The American military culture's efforts to expunge the specter of Vietnam, embodied in the mantra 'No More Vietnams,' also prevented the US Army as an institution from really learning from those lessons."[34]

There are lessons to be learned from Vietnam, including many relating to transnational sanctuary. The full range of issues relating to the tricky diplomatic problems of international frontiers and irregular warfare were fully on display. So, too, were the responses. As a wealthy and technologically advanced modern state, the United States had within its power the ability to attempt a wide variety of schemes to deny the communist enemy their transnational sanctuaries. The failures and successes among those efforts, coupled with a solid understanding of the successes and failures in the overall American effort, provide a variety of insights on the issue of transnational sanctuary in irregular warfare.

The same could be said of the Soviet war in Afghanistan (1979-1989). Although in hindsight it seems clear that the communist system of the Soviet Union was collapsing under its own weight by the 1980s, the Soviets had still amassed an enormous and technologically advanced military. Like the Americans before Vietnam, they had not invested much time or effort in developing counterinsurgency doctrine, so they had to play catch-up when the rebellion broke out in Afghanistan. And like the Americans, they tried a wide variety of techniques to stop insurgents from making use of their transnational sanctuary. But unlike the Americans, the Soviets had no compunctions whatsoever about using the most brutal techniques to put down an insurgency.

However, the Soviet war effort is not the focus of this case study. There is another perspective to the Soviet-Afghan War that is equally enlightening—the perspective of the insurgents. When it came to Afghanistan, the United States found itself in unfamiliar territory. For once, the Americans had a chance to provide the rebels with aid to fight their war against the communists. Those rebels and that American aid depended on access to transnational sanctuary. The development of that sanctuary, the

Soviet attempts to deny it, and the insurgent responses are all important topics in understanding how transnational sanctuaries can affect the outcome of insurgent wars.

There are no simple answers to fighting a successful counterinsurgency, no easy steps to victory. But a more thorough understanding of the problem and all of its dimensions can help shape sound policies, strategies, and tactics. Transnational sanctuary is an aspect in the global war on terrorism. This study explores that problem.

Endnotes

1. Richard W. Stewart, *The United States Army in Afghanistan: Operation Enduring Freedom* (Washington, DC: US Army Center of Military History, n.d.), 26-44.

2. "Pakistan Rejects US 'Right' to Incursions," *Los Angeles Times*, 5 January 2003, A4.

3. John Lancaster, "Pakistan Touts Control of Border," *Washington Post*, 2 September 2003, A10; David Rohde, "Pakistan: Border Toll Rises," *New York Times*, 18 March 2004, A17; Dana Priest and Kamran Khan, "Al-Qaeda Leaders May Be Cornered," *Washington Post*, 19 March 2004, A1; "Pakistan Says 50 Killed in Airstrike on Terror Camp," *Los Angeles Times*, 10 September 2004, A9.

4. John Lancaster, "Pakistan Rebuts Bin Laden Report," *Washington Post*, 8 March 2003, A19; David Johnson, "Search for Al-Qaeda Leader Focuses on Pakistan Border Area," *New York Times*, 8 March 2003; Gretchen Peters, "Bin Laden's Hideout in Wilds of Pakistan," *Christian Science Monitor*, 15 September 2003, 1; Mike Allen, "Afghan Worries Envoy; Incoming US Ambassador Seeks More Vigilance Along Pakistani Border," *Washington Post*, 19 November 2003, A22; Dana Priest, "US Aids Security of Musharraf," *Washington Post*, 3 January 2004, A1; and David Rohde, "G.I.'s in Afghanistan on Hunt," *New York Times*, 30 March 2004, A1.

5. Dafna Linzer and Griff White, "US Airstrike Targets Al-Qaeda's Zawahiri," *Washington Post*, 14 January 2006, A9; Zahid Hussain, "Political Fallout in Pakistan Strike Tests a US Ally," *Wall Street Journal*, 16 January 2006, A13; and Carlotta Gall, "Pakistanis Say US Raid Left 4 or 5 Militants Dead," *New York Times*, 18 January 2006, A6.

6. Zulfiqar Ali, "Musharraf Lashes Out at Karzai Over Data on Rebels," *Los Angeles Times*, 6 March 2006, A5; Calotta Gall, "2 Leaders Trade Barbs Over Fight Against Taliban," *New York Times*, 7 March 2006.

7. The Americans hoped that the invasion of Iraq would provide an implicit threat to the hostile regimes in Syria and Iran, especially. Bob Woodward, *Plan of Attack* (New York: Simon and Schuster, 2004), 90, 155, 231; and Michael R. Gordon and Bernard E. Trainor, *COBRA II: The Inside Story of the Invasion and Occupation of Iraq* (New York: Pantheon Books, 2006), 40, 73, 497.

8. Gregory Fontenot, et al., *On Point: The United States Army in Operation Iraqi Freedom* (Fort Leavenworth, KS: Combat Studies Institute Press, 2004), 145, 402; Tommy Franks, *American Soldier* (New York: HarperCollins, 2004), 352, 407-408, 414-415, 428-429, 500-501; Gordon and Trainor, *Cobra II*, 338, 450-454; Woodward, *Plan of Attack*, 147-148, 256-264, 324-325, 330, 368-370.

9. It is also possible, but unconfirmed, that the Iraqis moved weapons of mass destruction across the Syrian border before Coalition troops arrived. See Gordon and Trainor, *COBRA II*, 122, 132; and Georges Sada, *Saddam's Secrets: How an Iraqi General Defied and Survived Saddam Hussein* (Nashville, TN: Integrity Publishers, 2006).

10.   Gordon and Trainor, *COBRA II*, 489.

11.   Franks, *American Soldier*, 511.

12.   Fontenot, et al., *On Point*, 213, 249, 257, 279, 364, 367; Gordon and Trainor, *COBRA II*, 372, 408-409; 501 Franks, *American Soldier*, 519.

13.   Gordon and Trainor, *COBRA II*, 436.

14.   Quoted in Walter Pincus, "Syria Warned Again Not to 'Meddle' in Iraq," *Washington Post*, 11 April 2003, A37.

15.   L. Paul Bremer, *My Year in Iraq: The Struggle to Build a Future of Hope* (New York: Simon and Schuster, 2006), 104-105.

16.   Including launching Operation CHAMBERLAIN in October 2003. On these issues see Bay Fang, "Keeping an Eye on the Exit," *US News and World Report*, 134 (12 May 2003), 19; Dexter Filkins, "Conflict on Iraq-Syria Border Feeds Rage Against the US," *New York Times*, 15 July 2003, A1; and John Sattler, "Central Command Operations Briefing," 16 April 2004, United States Department of Defense News Transcript, online at http://www.defenselink.mil.

17.   Michael Linnington interview, conducted by Catherine Small, 3 November 2005, Fort Leavenworth, KS, in author's possession.

18.   Ibid. See also the letter from Colonel Linnington to Michael Rubin of National Review Online and Rubin's response, "Letters: Border Security and More," 13 May 2004, National Review Online, http://www.nationalreview.com, and Vernon Loeb, "Commanders Doubt Syria Is Entry Point," *Washington Post*, 29 October 2003, A19.

19.   David Teeples interview, conducted by Pete Connors, 4 November 2005, Fort Leavenworth, KS, in author's possession.

20.   Ibid.

21.   Ibid.; 3d Armored Cavalry Regiment, "Rifles Update Brief," n.d., in author's possession; and *Blood and Steel!: The History, Customs, and Traditions of the 3d Armored Cavalry Regiments* (Fort Carson, CO: Third Cavalry Museum, n.d.), 40-43.

22.   Tony Perry, "Marines Hunt Smugglers at Iraq-Syria Border," *Los Angeles Times*, 30 March 2004, A6; Melissa August, "Cozying Up To Syria," *Time*, 164 (27 September 2004), 17; Nora Boustany, "Syrian Sees Calming of Tension," *Washington Post*, 6 October 2004, A24; Johanna McGeary, "The Trouble With Syria," *Time*, 165 (28 February 2005), 30-31; Ellen Knickmeyer and Omar Fekeiki, "US Warplanes Target Alleged Rebel Havens Along Iraq-Syria Border," *Washington Post*, 31 August 2005, A18; Ashraf Khalil, "The Conflict in Iraq; Joint Force Targets Town Near Syria Border," 11 September 2005, A9; "20

Suspected Rebels Killed in Raids Near Syria Border," *Los Angeles Times*, 23 October 2005, A4; Thanassis Cambanis, "Syria Defends Efforts to Patrol Iraqi Border," *Boston Globe*, 29 October 2005; Howard LaFranchi, "Tougher International Line on Syria," *Christian Science Monitor*, 31 October 2005, 1; Michael Bruno, "McCain Pushes for Even More UAV Emphasis," *Aerospace Daily and Defense Report*, 217 (3 March 2006), 4.

23.   Then National Security Advisor Condoleezza Rice told a meeting of congressional leaders on the eve of the invasion, "We don't expect difficulties with Iran." Woodward, *Plan of Attack*, 370. See also Gordon and Trainor, *COBRA II*, 85.

24.   E.A. Torriero, "US Forces Act to Plug Iraq-Iran Border," *Chicago Tribune*, 13 May 2003.

25.   Bremer, *My Year in Iraq*, 71-73, 199, 274.

26.   Kim Murphy, "Securing Iraq's Frontier, Step by Step," *Los Angeles Times*, 30 March 2004, A6; and Rajiv Chandrasekaran and Karl Vick, "Iraq-Iran Border to Be Tightened in Bid to Stem Attacks," *Washington Post*, 14 March 2004, A26.

27.   John Ward Anderson, et al., "Bigger, Stronger Homemade Bombs Now to Blame for Half of US Deaths," *Washington Post*, 26 October 2005, A1.

28.   "IED Components Moving Across Iraq-Iran Border, General Says," *US Federal News Service*, 17 March 2006.

29.   Bernard B. Fall, *Street Without Joy* (Harrisburg, PA: Stackpole Books, 1967), 375.

30.   Although the use of sanctuaries also raises the likelihood of an expanded conflict. Idean Salehyan, "No Shelter Here: Rebel Sanctuaries and International Conflict," Paper for the American Political Science Association Meeting, Washington, DC, 2005.

31.   This discussion is heavily indebted to William Glenn Robertson, "The Active Sanctuary: Challenge to Counterinsurgency," 19 May 1969, unpublished paper, in author's possession. See also John D. Deiner, "Guerrilla Border Sanctuaries and Counterinsurgent Warfare," *Army Quarterly and Defense Journal*, 109 (April 1979), 162-179; G.R. Christmas, "Guerrilla Sanctuaries," *Infantry*, 63 (May-June 1973), 24-27.

32.   Paul Staniland, "Defeating Transnational Insurgencies: The Best Offense Is a Good Fence," *Washington Quarterly*, 29 (Winter 2005-06), 32; John R. Hamilton, "Defeating Insurgency on the Border," (Marine Corps Command and Staff College, 1985), Online: http://www.globalsecurity.org; and Joseph Jeremiah Zasloff, *The Role of Sanctuary in Insurgency: Communist China's Support to the Vietminh, 1946-1954* (Santa Monica, CA: RAND, 1967).

33.   Andrew J. Birtle, *US Army Counterinsurgency and Contingency Operations Doctrine* (Washington, DC: US Army Center of Military History, 2004); Keith B. Bickel, *Mars Learning: The Marine Corps Development of*

Small Wars Doctrine, 1915-1940 (Boulder, CO: Westview Press, 2001); Max Boot, *The Savage Wars of Peace: Small Wars and the Rise of American Power* (New York: Basic Books, 2002), xiii-285; Sam C. Sarkesian, *America's Forgotten Wars: The Counterrevolutionary Past and Lessons for the Future* (Westport, CT: Greenwood Press, 1984); United States Marine Corps, *Small Wars Manual – 1940* (Washington, DC: GPO, 1940); Lawrence M. Greenberg, *The Hukbalahap Insurrection: A Case Study of a Successful Anti-Insurgency Operation in the Philippines – 1946-1955* (Washington, DC: US Army Center of Military History, 1986); Larry Cable, "Reinventing the Round Wheel: Insurgency, Counter-Insurgency, and Peacekeeping Post Cold War," *Small Wars and Insurgencies*, 4 (Autumn 1993), 228-262; Brian McAllister Linn, "The Impact of the Imperial Wars (1898-1907) on the US Army," *Heritage Lectures*, 908 (14 November 2005), 2.

34. Robert M. Cassidy, "Back to the Street Without Joy: Counterinsurgency Lessons from Vietnam and Other Small Wars," *Parameters*, 34 (Summer 2004), 74.

Chapter 1
Vietnam

Indications

Shortly after midnight on 1 November 1964, a series of explosions shook the American air base at Bien Hoa. The attack dragged on for 20 minutes, and in that time more than fifty 81mm mortar rounds rained down on the airfield, barracks, and the parking areas for the various aircraft. The assault took the South Vietnamese and Americans who manned the field completely by surprise. By 1964, communist insurgents, known as the Vietcong to the Americans and their allies, had been wreaking havoc in South Vietnam for years, but they had never before launched a direct attack on an American target. The Americans never expected such a conventional assault. Base commanders considered sabotage the greater threat, so as a precaution, the B-57 bombers that had recently been brought in from the Philippines lined the field in the open. They were perfect targets for a mortar attack.

When the firing stopped, four Americans and two South Vietnamese were dead, and dozens of Americans and a handful of Vietnamese were wounded. Nearly 30 aircraft had been damaged to varying degrees, including 20 of the B-57 bombers. Five of the bombers had been completely destroyed, along with multiple helicopters. Ground troops and helicopters went out in a series of search parties to look for the Vietcong, but found only empty mortar canisters in a well-prepared position north of the base. The guerillas disappeared into the countryside.[1] Hanoi radio applauded the assault, calling it a major communist victory.[2] US Ambassador to South Vietnam Maxwell Taylor told policymakers in Washington that the attack was "a deliberate act of escalation."[3] In the days, weeks, and months that followed, the Vietcong launched more attacks, including the 6 February 1965 assaults on American installations at Pleiku. South Vietnam was on the verge of collapse.

The United States responded by stepping up its military role in Vietnam. The Air Force began a series of limited reprisal bombing missions over North Vietnam. Ground troops from the Army and Marine Corps were provided to defend vulnerable American airbases. Not yet satisfied, American policymakers in the spring and summer of 1965 made the fateful decision to send tens of thousands of additional ground troops to Vietnam. The major American entry into the war had begun—triggered by the actions of Vietcong guerillas in the winter of 1964-1965.[4] Yet the Vietcong had not done it alone.

By coincidence, the day before the attack on Bien Hoa, the US Military Assistance Command–Vietnam (MACV) completed a new study of insurgent infiltration of the South. It noted that the North Vietnamese had since 1959 directed and supplied the infiltration of tens of thousands of men and untold quantities of supplies into South Vietnam. The majority of the men and much of the material that made up the Vietcong, the report concluded, had crossed the border of South Vietnam from communist sanctuaries in Laos and Cambodia.[5]

Almost exactly one year after the guerrilla attack on Bien Hoa, a new threat emerged in the central highlands of South Vietnam. Vietnamese communists, flushed with their recent successes in guerilla warfare, decided that the time had come for a more direct approach. They planned to use the dry season of 1965-1966 to conquer the central highlands, split South Vietnam, and then use the captured territory as a staging point for future offensives. The problem for the communists was that US Army Special Forces were operating training and base camps along the Laotian and Cambodian border, including several on the central plateau. These camps were an irritant to the communist war effort and an impediment to the plan to conquer the highlands. In the fall of 1965, the North Vietnamese decided to act.

On 19 October 1965, the communists launched an assault on the Special Forces camp at Plei Me, 25 miles south of Pleiku. At first the Americans and South Vietnamese believed that the attack came from Vietcong insurgents, but within 48 hours it became clear that the communist forces were regiments of the North Vietnamese Army—conventional forces, not guerilas.[6] The defenders of Plei Me held out, due in no small part to massive air and artillery support, and an Army of the Republic of Vietnam (ARVN) relief column that fought through an ambush to relieve the base on 25 October. Their offensive broken, the North Vietnamese regiments retreated toward the Cambodian border.

Not content with the defensive victory, and anxious to try his preferred search and destroy tactics, General William Westmoreland, the commander of MACV, ordered a pursuit of the retreating forces by the recently arrived 1st Cavalry Division (Airmobile). After fighting a series of skirmishes,

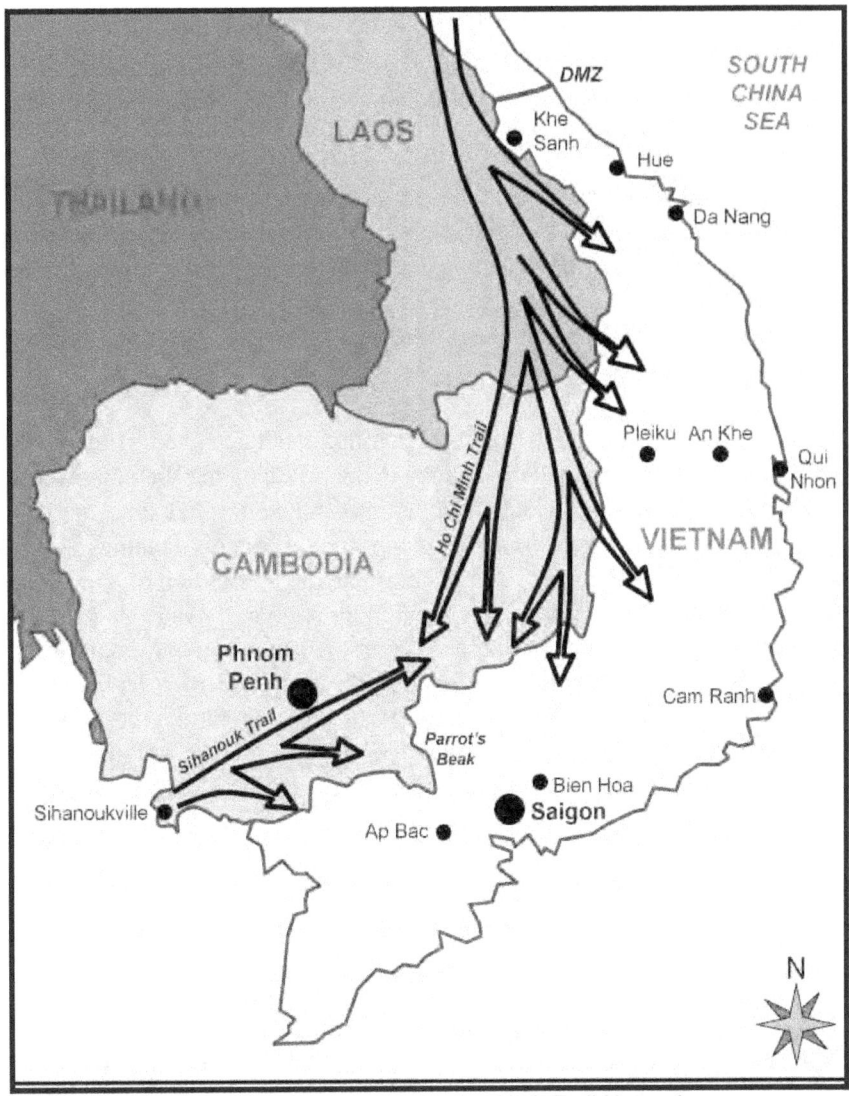

Map 1. Vietnam and the Ho Chi Minh Trail Network.

units from the 1st Cavalry Division made major contact with the NVA regiments just east of the Cambodian border in the Ia Drang Valley.

The NVA had decided to reconstitute their units and launch a division-size attack on Plei Me. On 14 November, unaware of enemy intentions, troops from the US Army 7th Cavalry Regiment landed near the new NVA staging area. A series of pitched battles in and around the American helicopter landing zones followed. Once again, the communists relied on surprise and aggression and the Americans leaned heavily on overwhelming air and artillery support. Both sides took heavy casualties and for a time it looked as if the American positions might be overrun. At the end of several days of brutal combat, both sides withdrew from the battlefields.

Afterward, fresh American and South Vietnamese troops moved into the area, but by then the North Vietnamese had retreated into Cambodia. Policy makers in Washington refused requests to pursue the enemy across the border. The campaign ended on 26 November. The devastated NVA division used the sanctuary to spend the next six months recovering from the battle.[7]

From the beginning, Vietnamese communists conceived of their war effort in two parts. First, the insurgency in the South by the Vietcong would weaken the ruling South Vietnamese regime and demoralize the American military. Second, a conventional campaign by the North Vietnamese Army would sweep through the South and complete the unification of Vietnam.[8] As a result, the Americans and South Vietnamese had to wage an effective counterinsurgency and be prepared to fight off larger conventional forces. America's first major battles in Vietnam, the attack on Bien Hoa and the fight in the Ia Drang Valley, indicated very early on the degree to which the communist war in Vietnam, unconventional and conventional, relied on sanctuary and supply across international borders. To defeat the communists, the Americans and their allies would have to deny that sanctuary.

The Dimensions of the Problem

The origins of the Vietnam War were in many ways complex, but they boiled down to a few simple issues. The United States was in the midst of the Cold War with Soviet- and Chinese-supported communism. Americans believed the lesson of World War II was aggression had to be stopped early, lest aggressors become strong and bold enough to force a world war. When Ho Chi Minh and his Vietnamese communist forces drove the French out of Indochina in 1954, Southeast Asia became one of the places where the United States had to stop aggression.

At the 1954 Geneva Conference, the great powers split Vietnam in two at a demilitarized zone (DMZ), roughly along the 17th parallel, and South Vietnam became a makeshift bulwark against the political or military spread of communism. For their part, Vietnamese communists, in

18

both North and South, would not accept the existence of an independent, noncommunist South Vietnam. They started an insurgency in the South against the South Vietnamese government of Ngo Dinh Diem. Eventually, the North Vietnamese planned to support the insurgency with conventional forces from the North.[9]

The United States made its primary strategic goal in Southeast Asia the preservation of a noncommunist South Vietnam. That goal meant providing for the security of South Vietnam.[10] There was no small amount of confusion and dissent among American and South Vietnamese leadership about how exactly to provide that security. Some saw conventional operations as key. Others focused on the counterinsurgency. Advocates of strategic airpower believed that bombing the North could win the war. From these competing ideas emerged a mishmash of operations and tactics that ultimately hindered the efforts to win the war.[11]

Operational and tactical clarity were further impeded by the fact that the North Vietnamese sent manpower, weapons, and supplies to the south by a variety of routes—by water, over the DMZ, and especially over the western borders of South Vietnam through Laos and Cambodia. It is hard to overstate the extent of the problem. While the impetus for the war itself came from North Vietnam, it was couched in the ideology of the communist world. That ideology had leadership in the competing powers of the Soviet Union and China. Both powers gave serious support to the Vietnamese communists during the war.

To make the problem worse, the North Vietnamese managed to play the Soviets and Chinese off one another, increasing the amount of aid they received from each. The Soviets gave billions of rubles in military assistance to North Vietnam, much of it in modern weaponry like planes, rockets, field artillery, surface to air missiles, and tanks. By 1968 roughly half of all aid to North Vietnam came from the Soviet Union.[12]

The Chinese accounted for much of the rest. Chinese sources indicate that between "1956 and 1963, China provided the DRV [the Democratic Republic of Vietnam, North Vietnam] with 270,000 guns, over 10,000 pieces of artillery, nearly 200 million bullets, 2.02 million artillery shells, 15,000 wire transmitters, over 1,000 trucks, 15 aircraft, 28 war ships, and 1.18 million sets of uniforms."[13] As the American role in Vietnam escalated, Mao Zedong responded by drastically increasing Chinese assistance to the North Vietnamese. This "massive supply of weapons to the DRV in 1962," argues historian Qiang Zhai, "helped Ho Chi Minh to intensify guerilla warfare in the South, triggering greater U.S. intervention."[14] With North Vietnamese engineers working on roads through Laos, well over 100,000 Chinese engineering troops flooded into North Vietnam to improve and expand the transportation network in the northern part of the country.[15] In that same period, the Chinese provided North Vietnam with approximately 1.5 million guns, 52,000 artillery pieces, 12 million artillery shells, millions of bullets and uniforms, and thousands of telephones, radio transmitters, and automobiles.[16] Throughout the conflict, Soviet and Chinese aid to North Vietnam went directly to the support of the insurgency in South Vietnam, freed up North Vietnamese resources to go south, or supplied the North Vietnamese Army directly.

The Soviets and Chinese provided an even more important aspect to the Vietnamese communist effort—the threat of direct intervention. American policymakers did not want another Korean War, so they went out of their way to avoid provoking Soviet or Chinese entry into the war. That decision meant that the United States never really threatened taking the ground war to North Vietnam. At the same time, the Soviet and Chinese threat gave the Vietnamese communists the ability to make a farce out of the nominal neutrality of Laotian and Cambodian territory.

In the American part of the war, the Vietnamese communists put all of these resources to good use. Vietnamese communists, having relied on Communist Chinese territory during the war with the French, had long experience with cross border sanctuaries.[17] The major infiltration of South Vietnam began when North Vietnamese forces crossed the DMZ in June 1959. The delivery routes, known to the communists as the "Truong Son Strategic Supply Route" and to the Americans as the Ho Chi Minh Trail, soon expanded to Laos. The Ho Chi Minh Trail ran through the Laotian panhandle and into Cambodia, along the western border of South Vietnam. It was later supplemented by the Sihanouk Trail, which ran northeast from the coast of southern Cambodia to various points along the western border of South Vietnam. The trails wound through the jungle, connected by various rest areas, aid stations, and supply dumps along the way. Porters carried supplies on their backs and walked heavily laden bicycles down the paths. As the trails developed, trucks carried heavier supplies, and armored units traveled south.

Most important of all were the men. At first, the trail allowed southerners to return to the South and join the Vietcong, but as the war escalated, more and more northerners went south to join the insurgency. During the course of the war, hundreds of thousands of Vietnamese went south to fight, most of them through Laos and Cambodia. Over time, the trail also became the route by which conventional NVA forces moved south to launch conventional attacks on South Vietnam, like the attack on Plei Me. When such units needed to rest and refit, they crossed the border and returned to larger resupply areas along the route. Such rear bases were extensive, consisting of artillery and surface to air missile positions, large storage bunkers, mess halls, training areas, and even farms to maintain crops and livestock. Later in the war, the communists moved the headquarters for the entire war effort in the south, the Central Office of South Vietnam (COSVN), to Cambodia.[18]

The South Vietnamese and their Americans allies recognized the problem from the beginning. As early as November 1960, American military advisers in Vietnam reported:

> The Viet Cong infiltrate into South Vietnam by use of overland trails through Laos and Cambodia.... To prevent this infiltration, the [Diem government] must have a firmer control of its frontiers. Frontiers which, because of the great length, ill-defined boundaries, and the nature of the terrain coupled with the political failure of the countries concerned to reach an agreement on policing of borders make the military task of preventing infiltration almost insurmountable....[19]

The struggle over sanctuary had begun, and it would drag on through the entire war. Indeed, as the leading historian of the Ho Chi Minh Trail writes, "In a very real sense the course of the Vietnam War became a competition between Hanoi's efforts to create and sustain an umbilical cord and American attempts to cut that cord or at least obstruct it."20

First Options

Unfortunately, diplomacy offered little help for the Americans and their allies. Both Laos and Cambodia were nominally neutral, but the signatories of the Southeast Asian Treaty Organization (SEATO) could not, or would not, come together to pressure the Vietnamese communists to respect that neutrality. Moreover, even the 1962 Geneva Accords that reaffirmed Laotian neutrality and removed foreign militaries did nothing to stop the communist efforts in the Laotian panhandle. The North Vietnamese never halted operation of the Ho Chi Minh Trail, and thousands of NVA and Vietcong remained in Laos. As one American official later commented, "North Vietnam broke the 1962 agreements before the ink was dry."21

The Americans were well aware of communist actions, but were hamstrung by the specter of Soviet or Chinese intervention.22 Still, the communist sanctuary in Laos and Cambodia could not be ignored. The North Vietnamese remained the preeminent force in the Laotian panhandle and eastern Cambodia, and that power gave them the opportunity to keep open the trails into South Vietnam. Diplomacy failed. The Americans needed a military solution that would fit inside the diplomatic framework of nominal Laotian and Cambodian neutrality, however one-sided that neutrality might be.

Given the tenuous diplomatic situation and the predilections of President John F. Kennedy and the major players in his administration, the first American military response made perfect sense. In military affairs, the Kennedy Administration relied on several rising stars to guide policy. Kennedy was particularly enamored of the ideas of General Maxwell Taylor. During the 1950s, Taylor had been a vocal opponent of President Dwight D. Eisenhower's strategic reliance on nuclear weapons. Taylor argued for expanded conventional forces with the capability to respond to a variety of threats, including insurgencies. Kennedy saw much merit in this line of thinking, and when he became president he quickly sought to expand America's Special Forces capabilities.23

Not surprisingly, Special Forces and other covert operators seemed to offer a solution to the sanctuary problem. As an added benefit, such units had been in Southeast Asia for years, acting as advisers for various friendly governments and militaries in the region.24 Beginning in 1961, the CIA and Army Special Forces worked together to initiate the Civilian Irregular Defense Group (CIDG) program. The CIDG organized and trained local ethnic groups like the Montagnards of the central highlands into defense forces to defeat the Vietcong in the backwater villages of Vietnam. Part of their mission was to screen the borders to prevent communist infiltration from Laos and Cambodia. As a result of their efforts, many of the most prominent Special Forces camps in South Vietnam, including the one at Plei Me, were opened in the period from 1961-1964.25

The early efforts of the CIA and Special Forces included limited attempts to interdict the supply lines within Laos. Starting in 1961, a few specially trained South Vietnamese teams launched infiltrations across the border to gather intelligence. The next year, CIA officers began training Lao natives in basic reconnaissance of the communist road system. Both programs gathered general information, but neither provided specifics on the communist operation.[26] A more direct approach came in 1964 when American advisers worked with South Vietnamese special forces on Operation LEAPING LENA. In LEAPING LENA, small teams of Montagnard tribesman led by South Vietnamese Special Forces were to cross into Laos to perform reconnaissance missions. In late June and early July 1964, five South Vietnamese teams parachuted into Laos. Their mission ended badly. The communists killed or captured all but a handful of the men, and those who survived had gathered little useable information.[27]

Despite the possible diplomatic ramifications of violating Laotian neutrality, leaders in the United States concluded from the failure of LEAPING LENA that Americans would have to play a direct part in future infiltrations of Laos. A move toward an expanded role for American Special Forces had already begun. In January 1964, the Americans set up the Studies and Observations Group (SOG) within MACV, a special operations group that answered directly to the Joint Chiefs of Staff. SOG included men from all of America's armed services, including Army Special Forces, Navy SEALs, and Air Force Air Commandos. SOG's mandate included operations into Laos, Cambodia, and North Vietnam.[28]

Infiltrations into Laos began in 1965, initially under the codename SHINING BRASS (in 1967 the name was changed to PRAIRIE FIRE). Operations in Cambodia, codenamed DANIEL BOONE, began in 1967. The teams included South Vietnamese troops led by American Special Forces personnel. Still concerned with violations of neutral territory, the men who went on these missions wore nondescript uniforms and carried untraceable weapons. They either crossed the border on foot or in unmarked Air Force helicopters, and similar helicopters would extract them at the end of missions.[29] In 1966 they sent more than 100 teams into Laos; two years later, some 800 teams went into Laos and Cambodia combined.[30]

SOGs primary task was reconnaissance, and in that role the troops provided important intelligence on the expansion of the Ho Chi Minh Trail in Laos and Cambodia. Special Forces troops took pictures of communist roads, bases, and equipment—all of which provided clear information on the extent of the sanctuary across the borders. Yet, they did more than observe. The teams engaged in all manner of small-scale combat operations, including destruction of enemy supplies, ambushes, and rescue missions.

They even captured communists and brought them to South Vietnam for interrogation. But the major part of their effort was to provide targeting for air strikes. In many cases, the infiltration teams would be accompanied by slow-flying planes that acted as forward air controllers for bombers.[31] Since the thick jungle concealed most targets, the men on the ground would radio the location of the enemy to the controllers, who would in turn call in the bombers. In January 1967, SOG troops even established a semi-permanent radio relay post on a mountaintop within Laos, called "Leghorn."[32]

Despite the skill, bravery, and individual effectiveness of these Special Forces infiltrations, in the end their effect on communist sanctuary was limited. One of the veterans of SOG recalled of the war on the Ho Chi Minh Trail, "You could pinprick it …. You could put a security requirement on the enemy by having him worry that there are people who are going to tear things up, take prisoners, direct air strikes, and so on but that's the most you could do with what you had then." He concluded, "I don't think SOG ever had the ability of stopping the trail flow."[33]

There were multiple reasons for the failure of the overall SOG effort to deny the communists sanctuary. For one thing, the Americans invested only limited resources in the effort, especially in comparison to the rest of the war. One estimate had the total cost of the missions from 1967-1969 at only $15.6 million.[34] Another problem was communist resistance. A participant in special operations activities later wrote that by 1970, the enemy knew exactly what the Special Forces were up to, and they began serious efforts to counter the Americans and South Vietnamese. As a result:

> The infiltration of recon teams from the Central Highlands launch sites into Cambodia and Laos was exceedingly dangerous. Infiltration from I Corps into Laos or into the DMZ region was near suicidal, but teams led by Special Forces volunteers continued the mission. HALO (high-altitude, low-opening) techniques, jumping into triple canopy jungle in smoke-jumper protective equipment, and blasting helicopter landing zones with huge bombs were among the methods used to get into denied areas. Stay-time in operational areas decreased as the enemy improved his detection, communication, tracking, and close combat skills. Despite brave men and stalwart staff efforts to stay ahead of the enemy, the tide had turned. By 1970 it is doubtful that the losses could be justified by the intelligence gained.[35]

Consequently, the number of SOG infiltrations into Laos and Cambodia began to decrease after 1969. Ultimately, Special Forces infiltrations into Laos and Cambodia had never been much more than a support mission for the largest American effort to destroy the cross border communist sanctuaries in the Vietnam War.

Airpower

From the moment humans took to the sky, military thinkers began theorizing about the impact of airpower on warfare. The most ardent proponents concluded that strategic bombing, if applied correctly, could win wars all on its own—without the horrible casualties of ground wars. At no time did this thinking hold more sway in the United States than in the years after World War II, when Americans looked to technology to solve the problems of the modern world. American policymakers in the Vietnam era were no exception to this rule. Secretary of Defense Robert McNamara led the way, drawing on his experiences in business and industry to conclude that there was a technological solution to every military problem and an equation to win any war. Kennedy may have had a fascination with Special Forces and unconventional war, but the men who made up his administration—and the man who succeeded him—had a near obsession with airpower. Such men gave little thought to applying that airpower to counterinsurgency and, for the duration of the war, advocated the full-scale bombing of North Vietnam.[36]

Not surprisingly, many of these same men, including President Lyndon Johnson, believed that airpower could interdict the communist line of supply in Laos and Cambodia—with the added benefit that airpower was more indirect than ground incursions, and therefore would not be as likely to draw the Chinese or Soviets into the war. Still, the Chinese and Soviet threat and nominal Laotian neutrality meant that initially Lao pilots bore the responsibility for bombing in Laos, which began in 1964 (working with American reconnaissance aircraft). Much like they had in LEAPING LENA, these proxy warriors failed to live up to American expectations, and by the end of the year, Johnson gave the go-ahead for the US Air Force to attack the communists trails and bases in Laos.[37]

Beginning with Operation BARREL ROLL in December 1964, the US Air Force and US Navy launched a series of escalating bombing missions against the communist infrastructure north of the DMZ in Laos. BARREL ROLL was supplemented by Operation STEEL TIGER in April 1965, but the latter began to spread the attacks to the eastern portion of the Laotian panhandle. Flying from bases in South Vietnam and Thailand, and off of carriers in the surrounding waters, American pilots flew nearly 800 missions against Laos in less than a month.[38] The airpower interdiction program accelerated in the summer and fall of 1965, as the Air Force started working with the SOG incursions and the targeting area extended south to the Cambodian border. In December, the Air Force used B-52 bombers to hit targets in Laos, most notably the Mu Gia pass just north of the DMZ. Even the aerial defoliant program, Operation RANCH HAND, spread into the eastern portion of the Laotian panhandle. The Americans flew some 3,000 attack sorties against Laos in December, a number that would rise to 8,000 in January 1966.

Most of these early attacks had been bombing missions by fast-moving jets, but in early 1966 the Air Force sent night raids by propeller driven AC-47 gunships to attack the communist roads and sanctuaries. The AC-47s enjoyed some success, but the enemy quickly adjusted tactics and the Americans had to replace the vulnerable gunships with the faster and more durable B-26K bomber (also known as the A-26A and A-26K). In the meantime, the operational area expanded to include targets throughout most of the Laotian panhandle.[39]

In all cases, politicians, including President Johnson and Ambassador to Laos William Sullivan, imposed restrictions on targets in Laos. Sullivan's actions in particular frustrated military commanders so much that General Westmoreland reported that they sometimes called the Ho Chi Minh Trail "Sullivan's Freeway."[40] That said, the American air campaign was significant. American pilots flew over 100,000 bombing missions to Laos and dropped hundreds of thousands of tons of ordnance on the trail in the years 1965-1967. Yet the infiltration continued, even accelerated, in those years. At least 12,000 North Vietnamese entered the South in 1964; in 1967, the number was at least 52,000 and possibly as many as 83,000.[41] Army officers recognized the depth of the problem, as indicated by a 1967 article in *Army Quarterly and Defense Journal*:

> Intense bombing of the Ho Chi Minh Trail has reduced the volume of traffic along it greatly, curtailed supplies, caused hunger and hardship, but has failed to close it completely. Continued bombing may further reduce movement, but absolute interdiction may not be achieved by this method as long as Viet Cong determination and morale can stand the strain. The lesson seems to be that air power can delay, harass and destroy, but alone it cannot accomplish the desired objective.[42]

The failure of the bombing to stop major infiltrations into South Vietnam or deny sanctuary in Laos and Cambodia became perfectly clear in early 1968. On 21 January, the Marine base at Khe Sanh in the northern province of Quang Tri, less than 10 miles from the border of Laos, came under heavy attack from NVA forces. The communists, attacking from Laos, used a full array of conventional weapons to assault the hilltop fort. In one of the most direct exploitations of sanctuary, the NVA even shelled Khe Sanh from artillery positions over the border. The marines held out, aided by airpower and their own artillery support, but the siege dragged on until April, indicating the strength of the NVA support system in Laos.[43]

Even more shocking was the general Vietcong Tet Offensive, beginning 29-30 January 1968. During the New Year's Tet holiday, the Vietcong launched a massive assault on towns and cities throughout South Vietnam. Despite some early communist successes, most famously at the American embassy in Saigon and in the northern city of Hue, the allied forces beat back the Vietcong at every turn. The communists took horrendous casualties, which dealt a serious blow to the insurgency in the South. Nevertheless, the scope of the conventional attack on Khe Sanh and the guerrilla assaults of Tet belied any claims that the allied effort to stop communist infiltration of the South through Laos and Cambodia had been successful.[44]

Aware of the failure to deny sanctuary so far, but undeterred in their confidence that the proper application of airpower could do the job, American policy makers forged ahead with their plans to interdict the Ho Chi Minh Trail. They had already initiated a new plan for 1968, one that would rely even more heavily on technology to solve the problem. Inspired by the success of the French in building a denial barrier during the war in Algeria, Americans sought to borrow from the concept.[45] In 1966 the idea of building some sort of barrier at the DMZ and in Laos came to the attention of Secretary of Defense McNamara. Later that year, a scientific advisory group concluded that the United States could deny the infiltration of South Vietnam by using electronic sensors to detect the enemy. The Secretary of Defense embraced the idea, and the concept of the electronic barrier became known as the McNamara Line. The Defense Department set up an independent and well-funded planning group to develop the systems, which were ready by the end of 1967. The military planned to deploy acoustic and seismic sensors—along with mines, bomblets, and bombs— all along key infiltration routes at the DMZ and into Laos. Fast-moving aerial and ground strike teams would respond to sensor hits to attack the infiltrators. Such systems performed well when diverted to the defense around Khe Sanh in early 1968, so there was reason to hope.[46]

In truth, the McNamara Line plan never had a chance. Well before the arrival of the sensor equipment, Westmoreland converted the line at the DMZ to more of a traditional series of defensive positions, to be manned by ARVN troops and US Marines in that sector. The line would run parallel to the DMZ, and consist of a cleared area roughly one half mile wide, "containing barbed wire, minefields, sensors, and watchtowers backed by a series of manned strongpoints. Behind the point would be a series of fire support bases to provide an interlocking pattern of artillery fire."[47] The Marines resented the mission because it limited their tactical flexibility, and they took serious casualties in the process of building the line.[48] As 1968 dragged on, and with attention and materials focused on Khe Sanh and Tet, the construction of the line fell far behind schedule. Where the sensors did get put into use, they did not stop infiltration, and the military halted construction of the barrier along the DMZ.

A greater test of the use of the electronic battlefield to stop infiltration came with its extension into Laos. The operations, codenamed MUSCLE SHOALS and IGLOO WHITE, placed the full array of sensors, bomblets, and mines on the supposed locations of the communist trails in Laos. Planes dropped most of the sensors, but Special Forces units also delivered some of the sensitive devices. The electronic battlefield had two targets: men and vehicles, specifically trucks. The antipersonnel system involved the use of small bomblets that, when stepped on and detonated, would be detected by acoustic sensors. Gravel antipersonnel mines often went along with the bomblets, and could disable a man if he stepped on them. The seismic sensors could pick up trucks from the vibrations they made as they rumbled over jungle roads. In either case, a circling aircraft would pick up the sensor data and call in fighters, bombers, or gunships to destroy the enemy.[49]

IGLOO WHITE coincided with an escalated air campaign against Laos and, eventually, Cambodia. The various COMMANDO HUNT operations of 1968-1972 attacked roads, terrain features, trucks, and antiaircraft positions and relied heavily on the electronic sensors to find targets. The bombing extended into Cambodia in March 1969, but used high altitude B-52 bombers to maintain the illusion of Cambodian neutrality. The operations in Laos paid special attention to interdicting trucks on the Ho Chi Minh Trail, and gunships, such as the new AC-130, and new night vision scopes did much of the damage. The operators of this 'war against trucks' claimed that they inflicted enormous destruction upon the communist logistic system, including destroying tens of thousands of trucks.[50]

There was some truth to their claim. Overall, airpower alone account-ed for over half of all of the billions of dollars the United States spent on Vietnam, and a large portion of those resources went toward denying cross border sanctuaries. American pilots dropped more than three million tons of bombs on Laos during the war; three times as much as on North Viet-nam.[51] All of that firepower had to have some effect. There was no doubt that the bombing was doing some damage to the communist war effort, but not nearly enough to deny the communists their bases and trails in Laos and Cambodia. As many as 600,000 NVA went south from 1966-1971. By North Vietnamese estimates, "in 1969 Hanoi lost to air attacks 13.5 percent of the tonnage it sent south; the figure was 3.4 percent in 1970 and 2.07 percent in 1971."[52]

Airpower failed for a variety of reasons. First, the communists used nature well. One American who managed to visit the trail in Laos in 1965 explained the problem: "The 'trail,' even in this rainy season was a thor-oughly passable road. We drove two jeeps over it for more than a mile. It would have easily accommodated 4x4 trucks. Yet nowhere on this road, except for two very limited areas, was it open to the sky. Even flying over it slowly with a helicopter, the road was not discernable from above."[53] The NVA camouflaged their vehicles and bases and recognized which targets the Americans were forbidden to attack and built their facilities around those targets. As the war went on, they built increasingly complex antiaircraft positions that made it harder for the Americans to linger over key communist positions. They waged a relentless war on American sen-sors and mines using explosives and simple tools like poles, shovels, and ropes.[54] The communists put thousands of manual laborers to good use re-building or bypassing damaged portions of the trail at night. In this effort, they took advantage of American firepower by using the rubble, especially gravel, left over by bombs to build simple bridges and fords. As one for-mer Vietcong recalled, "Over years this resulted in a web of bypasses and cutoffs, which made the system practically invulnerable to attack."[55]

Also important was the fact that the communists did not need a lot of resources to keep up the insurgency in the South. Individuals avoided de-tection much easier than equipment, and before 1968, the Vietcong could rely on sanctuaries and resources inside South Vietnam. The regular NVA forces in Laos and Cambodia required more support down the trail, but they never suffered any sustained shortages either. Part of the reason was that the sanctuary covered so much territory. But more important was the fact that for most of the war, the communists controlled the pace of ground operations. When American air interdiction damaged the enemy logistic system, the NVA could hoard supplies until the American pressure lifted. Airpower could do little or nothing to change this equation.56 And still the problem of sanctuary remained and would continue even when the nature of the war changed after 1968.

Pacification and Ground Incursions

From the outset of the war, some Americans had suggested an approach that focused first on defeating the insurgency in South Vietnam. They saw the war as a struggle for the hearts and minds of the people in the South, a struggle that the communists were winning.[57] By the time the Americans entered the war in large numbers, the Vietcong had gained de facto control of large areas within the South. They used these areas as re-supply and staging points for operations throughout the country. Some of the larger base areas were in the north near Khe Sanh and west of Hue, in the central plateau southwest of Pleiku, dotted around Saigon in the south, and in the extreme southern tip of the country.

The communists enjoyed this success in the South in large part because they employed terror techniques on the population. They eliminated resistance in villages through intimidation and brutal violence. In his study of the Ho Chi Minh trail, John Prados describes how the Vietcong dealt with the opposition from local landlords early on in the war: "The landlords were beheaded as an example to others. After that, the Viet Cong could come and go as they pleased...."[58] At the same time, Vietcong units regularly threw grenades into crowds and vehicles, fired small arms into villages at night, assassinated and kidnapped village leaders and teachers, and burned down sections of villages. The Americans estimated that in 1965 alone over 12,000 civilians were kidnapped or killed as part of some 36,000 attacks on the Vietnamese people.[59] It did not help that early on in the war, the Americans and the various inefficient South Vietnamese regimes did little to earn the trust of the village population in the South. Instead of protecting them from the Vietcong, they rounded up the villagers into concentration camps called strategic hamlets, or did great damage to villages with indiscriminate or unobserved bombing or bombardment.[60]

The Tet Offensive and the follow up Vietcong assaults of the summer of 1968 gave the allies a new chance in the war against the insurgents. The bloody battles nearly destroyed the Vietcong in the South, and they provided the justification and motivation for the South Vietnamese to begin a general mobilization.[61] That summer, General Creighton Abrams replaced Westmoreland as the commander of MACV. Abrams appreciated the chance he had to defeat the insurgency from within, and working with Ambassador Ellsworth Bunker and the CIA's William Colby, he developed the transition away from search and destroy missions toward clear and hold efforts. The idea was to pacify the countryside, weed out local insurgents, protect the villagers, and thereby deny the communists sanctuary within South Vietnam. The political situation at home demanded that the Americans begin to withdraw ground troops from Vietnam, so this pacification program became a part of the larger effort of turning the war over to the South Vietnamese called Vietnamization.[62]

To a large degree, Abrams and the Americans were successful in the effort to clear South Vietnam of communist sanctuaries, but as they did so, it became all the more apparent how much the communists were relying on their rear area bases in Laos and Cambodia.[63] In 1969 and 1970, Vietcong and NVA units in South Vietnam either operated at only a small fraction of their authorized strength, or they were forced to retreat back to Laotian and Cambodian sanctuaries. Yet Hanoi continued to supply these units and launch attacks from across the border as the American air attacks had little effect on these communist efforts.[64] So even as the counterinsurgency showed signs of succeeding, the Americans felt compelled to make yet another attempt to destroy the sanctuaries in Cambodia and Laos.[65]

For years, American military commanders on the ground in Vietnam wanted to take the war to the communists. They would have preferred to send ground troops into North Vietnam and end the war by defeating the communists at home. At the very least, they wanted regular ground troops to have the ability to pursue the NVA and Vietcong into their sanctuaries in Laos and Cambodia.[66] The possibility of Chinese or Soviet intervention made such moves impossible for most of the war. The situation changed in 1970. That year President Richard Nixon gave the okay for American troops to cross into Cambodia.

As a candidate for the presidency in 1968, Nixon had promised peace with honor in Vietnam. True to his word as president, he facilitated the withdrawal of American forces. But keeping honor meant being willing to expand the war even as the troops withdrew. In the spring of 1970, the unstable political situation in Cambodia had led the NVA to try to take over the country. Cambodia was troublesome enough as a covert communist sanctuary; the United States could not tolerate the neighboring country becoming an open proxy to the North Vietnamese. In April, the order came down to go after the communist sanctuaries along the border in Cambodia.[67]

The attacks began in late April 1970 with ARVN units going in first. Although by orders the allies could only penetrate to a depth of roughly 20 miles, the incursions resembled a general offensive in that they extended all along the Cambodian border. Beginning in early May, the US 4th Infantry Division and ARVN forces made smaller assaults across the border from the central highlands area, roughly in the vicinity of Pleiku. These units captured some NVA supply caches and fought a number of small clashes. In the south in the Mekong delta region, ARVN units supported by riverine vessels of the US and Vietnamese navies advanced as far as Phnom Penh and repatriated tens of thousands of Vietnamese refugees' Psychological operations also played a role. American planes dropped leaflets over Cambodia to inform communist troops "the hitherto so-called 'sanctuaries' of yours on Cambodian territories are being levelled [sic] by massive operations of the combined Vietnamese-American forces." Another leaflet announced "save yourself from this onslaught—surrender!"[69]

The primary allied assaults came in the center, and were aimed at the alleged locations of larger NVA caches—and the supposed location of COSVN—in the areas along the border known as Fishhook, Dog's Head, and Parrot's Beak west and northwest of Saigon. A mixed American and ARVN force moved into the area of Parrot's Beak and found and destroyed a small communist base, but the area was not as essential to NVA activities as the Dog's Head and southern portion of the Fishhook farther north.

On the morning of 1 May 1970, bombing by B-52s and an extended artillery barrage prepared the way for the attack. ARVN airborne battalions landed in the Fishhook to try to cut off NVA retreats. In the meantime, a mixed collection of American cavalry, armored cavalry, and mechanized infantry called Task Force *Shoemaker* moved in from the south. The communists did retreat, taking significant casualties in the process, and the American advance sealed off the Fishhook.[70] The allies began looking for supply caches and found a major base that had belonged to the North Vietnamese 7th Division:

> Covering more than 1.2 square miles, the base contained over five hundred structures, many of them storage houses filled with more than two hundred tons of rice. Bamboo walkways linked rows of barracks with a sprawling hospital, mess

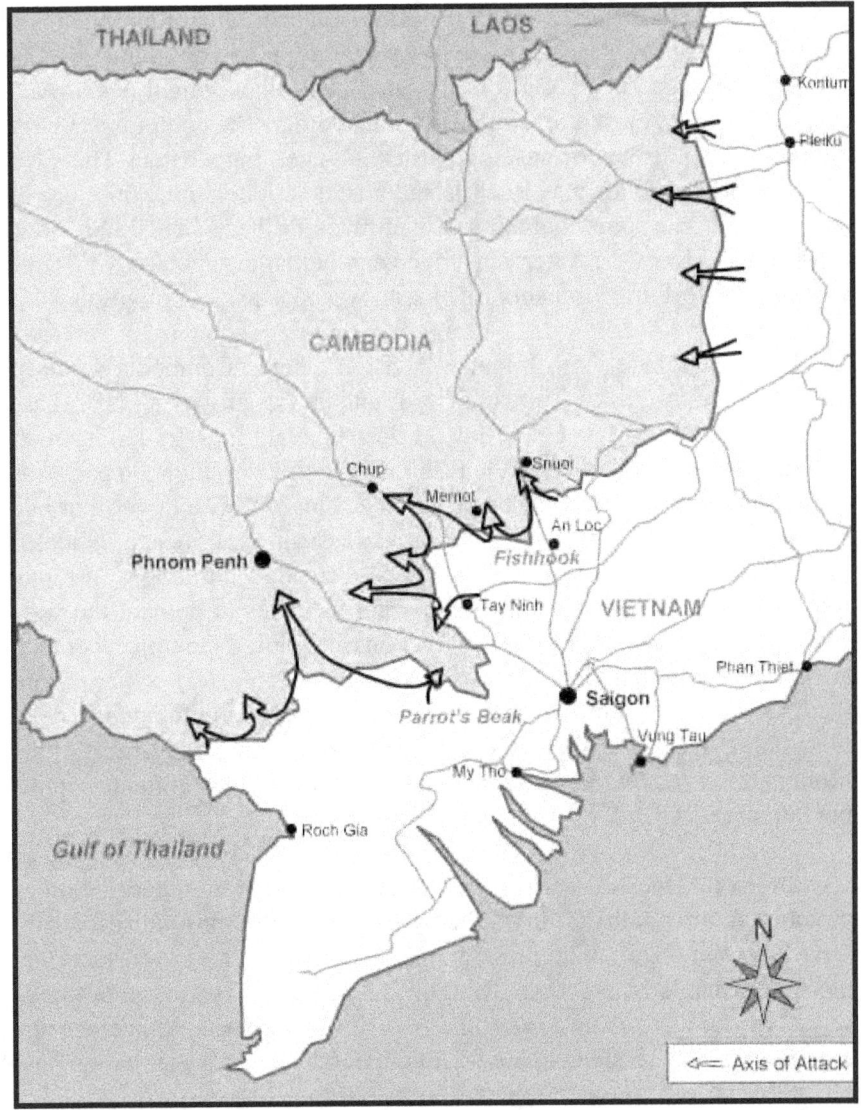

Map 2. The 1970 Cambodia Incursions.

compound, and a training area. There was even a sunken clay swimming pool surrounded by bamboo lounge chairs. Awed by the complex's sheer size, troopers quickly dubbed it "The City."[71]

Over the next several days, the Americans transported over 200 tons of weapons, ammunition, mines, explosives, and rice back to Vietnam, and destroyed another 40 tons of materiel rather than leave it behind.[72]

On 6 May 2d Brigade, 1st Cavalry Division attacked north of the Fishhook. From the onset, their mission was to find more communist supply caches. They succeeded. On 8 May, American troops fought a sharp action with the NVA just a few miles from the border. The communists were defending another enormous supply depot—even bigger than The City. This one became known as Rock Island East, and it held over 300 tons of supplies and weapons, including Soviet-made artillery shells and a few trucks. On 23 May, the Americans found another large depot; only this one consisted of 59 buried bunkers filled with weapons and ammunition.[73]

The 1st Brigade, 25th Infantry Division entered Cambodia south of the Fishhook on 6 May. They quickly found and destroyed an NVA base area and left by 14 May. On 9 May 2d Brigade, 25th Infantry Division attacked the southern portion of the Fishhook. Their assignment, in part, was to find and destroy COSVN headquarters, a high profile target that had been missed in the Task Force *Shoemaker* assault. Intelligence indicated that the headquarters was to the east of 2d Brigade's initial assault route. Expecting a stiff fight, the Americans sent in B-52s to prepare the way. The Americans encircled the NVA positions and closed the trap. Everyone at MACV knew that COSVN was not based in some sort of permanent facility, and indeed a month earlier most of COSVN had retreated to positions farther inside Cambodia. The Americans overran the remnants of the headquarters, destroying staff sections such as the postal and finance units, but not all of COSVN.[74]

Afterward, the NVA withdrew deeper into Cambodia, and the allies swept the border areas clean of supply caches. With monsoon season approaching and the 30 June presidential deadline for withdrawal looming, the Americans left Cambodia. Roughly, 34,000 South Vietnamese troops stayed on for a few weeks after the Americans departed. Altogether, the two months of incursions involved roughly 60,000 South Vietnamese and 50,000 American troops. Estimates vary, but the allies probably killed at least 10,000 NVA and Vietcong. They captured or destroyed tens of thousands of weapons, 1,800 tons of ammunition, over 8,000 tons of rice, and over a million pages of documents. Roughly, 1,200 allied troops died in the effort, including over 400 Americans. The attacks hurt communist morale, cut off the Sinahouk Trail, and set back NVA efforts on the border for months, but did not deny the NVA sanctuary altogether in Cambodia, nor did the attacks deal with the Ho Chi Minh Trail and sanctuaries in Laos.[75]

American forces continued to withdraw from South Vietnam after the incursion, but the South Vietnamese, bolstered by the success of the attacks into Cambodia and warned of an impending NVA offensive, launched a more ambitious cross border attack early the next year. This time the target was Laos, and all of the ground forces would be South Vietnamese—supported by a massive American logistics effort.[76] Codenamed LAM SON 719, the plan was to attack west from the area of Khe Sanh toward the key Laotian road junction at Tchepone. From there they would temporarily cut the Ho Chi Minh Trail, destroy communist supply depots in the area, and then return to South Vietnam. The South Vietnamese sent in their best and most seasoned units, including the 1st Infantry Division, the airborne division, the 1st Armored Brigade Task Force, the marine division, and ranger units.

On 8 February 1971, the South Vietnamese began their attack with armored units leading the way. At first, the ARVN units made significant progress down Route 9, the rough road leading to Tchepone. However, the NVA knew they were coming and had prepared accordingly. By then the communist operation in Laos had been going on for more than a decade, and they had become very good at their job. The South Vietnamese faced a conventional army of at least 40,000 men, including multiple armored units with Soviet tanks and well-developed antiaircraft positions. Sustained NVA attacks, particularly along the northern portion of the incursion corridor, stalled the offensive about halfway to the objective by 18 February. The South Vietnamese settled down into brutal fighting, with the Americans flying air support.

In early March, ARVN renewed its efforts to reach Tchepone—this time by using American helicopters to airlift ARVN infantry to a series of linked landing zones all the way to the objective. Within a few days, they reached the outskirts of the city and inflicted heavy casualties on the NVA. Nevertheless, communist counterattacks picked up all along the ARVN salient and the South Vietnamese decided to withdraw from Laos earlier than planned. Even though most South Vietnamese units fought hard, the withdrawal was not sufficiently planned, and it turned into a near-rout. Americans continued to provide air support, and almost all of the ARVN forces were out of Laos by the end of March.[77]

Even though ARVN took heavy casualties, its armor and artillery underperformed, it left behind too much equipment and materiel during the retreat, and some of the South Vietnamese leadership bickered and acted indecisively, LAM SON 719 was not a total failure. The South Vietnamese troops fought hard and, with the aid of American air power, inflicted serious damage on the NVA in Laos. Communist operations in South Vietnam slowed significantly for the rest of 1971.78 But the operation, like the effort in Cambodia the year before, had neither permanently cut the Ho Chi Minh Trail nor denied the communists refuge across the border. In the end, the relatively limited Cambodian and Laotian incursions of 1970-1971 did less to solve the problem than to show the extent of NVA operations and sanctuaries across the borders.79

Ending the War

By the end of 1971, there were only 139,000 US troops left in South Vietnam; with another 70,000 slated to leave by 1 May. In the meantime, the communists stepped up their efforts in Laos and Cambodia.[80] As the insurgency collapsed in South Vietnam and the Americans withdrew, the communists increasingly used their cross border sanctuaries to prepare for a conventional invasion. The changing nature of the war could be seen in the aid to the communists. Prior to 1970, China provided the North Vietnamese with only a handful of tanks and automobiles, but after 1970, Chinese supplies increasingly included weapons for conventional warfare. The years between 1970 and 1972 saw a drastic increase in the numbers of tanks, artillery pieces, and automobiles provided by the Chinese.[81] In turn, the North Vietnamese managed to get many of these weapons down the Ho Chi Minh trail into Laos and Cambodia.

In the spring of 1972, they put those resources to use. NVA general Vo Nguyen Giap believed that the NVA's armor and artillery superiority would prove decisive in his planned conventional invasion to end the war. As he said in a speech in December 1971, "Victory is in sight."[82] The Easter Offensive began on 30 March 1972 with a massive attack across the DMZ. Two other assaults followed right behind, one in the central highlands initiated from southern Laos and northern Cambodia, and another out of the Fishhook region of the Cambodian border. By the end of the battle, Giap would commit almost all of his forces, including over 11 divisions and nearly 30 independent infantry and artillery regiments.

In the north, ARVN, American advisers, and heavy American aerial bombing and naval bombardment were successful in slowing the communist advance so that it did not take Quang Tri City until 1 May. In a bloody campaign, the South Vietnamese held the line before Hue, launched a counteroffensive, and recaptured most of Quang Tri province by the end of the summer. Similar campaigns were fought throughout the country. After initial setbacks, ARVN maintained control of the key cities of Kontum in the central highlands and Ap Bac northwest of Saigon. Counteroffensives recaptured much, though not all, of the lost territory. In all cases, heavy American bombing—including the use of B-52s and newly designed laser-guided bombs—proved essential to the South Vietnamese effort. The Easter Offensive represented a massive loss for the NVA. They suffered at least 100,000 casualties, including at least 40,000 killed. In addition, they lost all manner of weapons and depleted their supply reserves. Even General Giap relinquished his command.[83]

The aftermath of the offensive saw a renewed effort by the Americans to complete their withdrawal. By the end of the year, the major parties in the war negotiated the Paris Peace Accords, which were signed in January 1973. The Americans all but completed their withdrawal from South Vietnam by March, leaving only a handful of advisors and diplomats. Congress cut off American aid to South Vietnam in August. The North Vietnamese immediately renewed their efforts. Once again, they used the Laotian and Cambodian sanctuaries to rest and refit. They funneled supplies and men south and prepared to begin yet another attack on the South. In 1974, they launched a series of strategic raids throughout the South. Buoyed by the success of these raids, they launched a massive final offensive on 10 March 1975. The largest attacks came from Laos and Cambodia. Without American support, ARVN collapsed. South Vietnam fell by May.[84]

The United States failed to preserve an independent noncommunist South Vietnam for several reasons. The Americans leaned too heavily on technology, hoping that airpower would coerce the communists to give up the fight. American military commanders on the ground early on did not appreciate the nature of the communist war, and tended to focus too heavily on the conventional aspects. They came around to the insurgency later, and then did not focus enough on the conventional threats. The communists won the war of public opinion, so that after Tet the war became a waiting game until the Americans left. For their part, the South Vietnamese improved but never developed a competent and corrupt-free government and military.

But even if the Americans from the beginning had developed a sound strategy, understood the dimensions of the insurgent and conventional threats, fought an effective public opinion battle, and got the South Vietnamese to govern and fight with efficiency and alacrity, they still would have had to come to grips with the problem of transnational sanctuary in Laos and Cambodia. The communists took a long view of the war, both as an insurgency and a conventional affair. As long as they could rest, refit, and launch attacks from relatively secure sanctuaries, they could control the pace of operations and maintain the ability to fight almost indefinitely. When asked in 1995 how the Americans could have won the war, former NVA colonel Bui Tin replied simply, "Cut the Ho Chi Minh trail inside Laos."[85] The communist war effort hinged on sanctuary—they could not have won without it.

Endnotes

1. "USMACV Military Report, 31 Oct to 7 Nov 64," Virtual Vietnam Archive, Texas Tech University, online at http://www.vietnam.ttu.edu, accessed 2 March 2006; Roger P. Fox, *Air Base Defense in the Republic of Vietnam, 1961-1973* (Washington, DC: Office of Air Force History, 1979), 1, 9, 16-17; Stanley Karnow, *Vietnam: A History* (New York: Viking, 1983), 401-403; and William C. Westmoreland, *A Soldier Reports* (Garden City, NY: Doubleday, 1976), 88-89.

2. "Vietnam Checklist for the DCI," 2 November 1962, Virtual Vietnam Archive, accessed 2 March 2006.

3. Taylor to Department of State, 1 November 1964, *Foreign Relations of the United States [FRUS]: Vietnam, 1964, vol. I* (Washington DC: GPO, 1992), 873.

4. Worries about repeated attacks on the order of Bien Hoa and the appropriate American response are spelled out in multiple areas. See *FRUS, Vietnam 1964, vol. I*, 873-888; *The Pentagon Papers (Gravel Edition), vol. III* (Boston: Beacon Press, 1971), 587-604; U.S. Grant Sharp, *Strategy for Defeat: Vietnam in Retrospect* (San Rafael, CA: Presidio Press, 1978), 48-49; Bruce Palmer, *The 25-Year War* (Lexington: University Press of Kentucky, 1984), 35-38; Andrew F. Krepinevich, *The Army and Vietnam* (Baltimore, MD: Johns Hopkins University Press, 1986), 97-99; Philip B. Davidson, *Vietnam at War: The History: 1946-1975* (Novato, CA: Presidio Press, 1988), 323-346; and George C. Herring, *America's Longest War: The United States and Vietnam, 1950-1975*, 3d ed. (New York: McGraw Hill, 1996), 137-150.

5. "Infiltration Study, Viet Cong Forces, Republic of Vietnam," 31 October 1964, *FRUS: Vietnam, 1964, vol. I*, 864-872.

6. "Operations Report–Lessons Learned, 3-66–The Pleiku Campaign," 4 May 1966, Virtual Vietnam Archive, accessed 8 March 2005.

7. Ibid., "After Action Report, Ia Drang Valley Operation, 1st Battalion, 7th Cavalry," 9 December 1965, in author's possession; George C. Herring, "The 1st Cavalry and the Ia Drang Valley, 18 October-24 November 1965," in *America's First Battles, 1776-1965*, eds. Charles E. Heller and William A. Stofft, (Lawrence: University Press of Kansas, 1986), 300-326; John A. Cash, "Fight at the Ia Drang," in *Seven Firefights in Vietnam*, eds. John A. Cash, John Albright, and Allan W. Sandstrum, (Washington, DC: Center of Military History, 1985), 3-40; John M. Carland, *Combat Operations: Stemming the Tide, May 1965 to October 1966* (Washington, DC: Center of Military History, 2000), 113-150; Harold G. Moore and Joseph L. Galloway, *We Were Soldiers Once...And Young* (New York: Random House, 1992).

8. Randall N. Briggs, "Compound Warfare in the Vietnam War," in *Compound Warfare: That Fatal Knot*, edited by Thomas M. Huber, (Fort Leavenworth, KS: US Army Command and General Staff College Press, 2002), 221-265.

9. John M. Gates, "People's War in Vietnam," *Journal of Military History*, 54 (July 1990), 326-330.

10. This simple statement of American strategy in Vietnam was spelled out on 17 March 1968 in National Security Action Memorandum 288. Herring, *America's Longest War*, 130-131. John Gates makes the salient point that South Vietnam, "was not a state to be defended but a state to be created." Gates, "People's War," 331. See also William J. Duiker, *Sacred War: Nationalism and Revolution in a Divided Vietnam* (New York: McGraw Hill, 1995), 95-137. The literature on the origins of the war is extensive and beyond the scope of this study. One excellent recent study is Frederik Logevall, *Choosing War: The Lost Chance for Peace and the Escalation of War in Vietnam* (Berkeley: University of California Press, 1999).

11. Alexander S. Cochran, "American Planning for Ground Combat in Vietnam, 1952-1965," *Parameters*, 14 (Summer 1984), 63-69.

12. Herring, *America's Longest War*, 163-164; Ilya V. Gaiduk, "The Vietnam War and Soviet-American Relations, 1964-1973: New Russian Evidence," *Cold War International History Project Bulletin*, 6-7 (Winter 1995-1996), 250-252.

13. Qiang Zhai, "Beijing and the Vietnam Conflict, 1964-1965: New Chinese Evidence," *Cold War International History Project Bulletin*, 6-7 (Winter 1995-1996), 234. See also Chen Jian, "China's Involvement in the Vietnam War, 1964-1969," *China Quarterly*, 142 (June 1995), 359.

14. Qiang, "Beijing and the Vietnam Conflict," 234; Chen, "China's Involvement," 358-364; and Xiaoming Zhang, "The Vietnam War, 1964-1969: A Chinese Perspective," *Journal of Military History*, 60 (October 1996), 732-736.

15. Over 150,000 Chinese antiaircraft artillery troops joined the effort. Chen, "China's Involvement," 364-377; Xiaoming, "Vietnam War," 755-756. During the major American portion of the war, from 1965 to 1973, over 320,000 Chinese troops of one sort or another served in North Vietnam. Qiang, "Beijing and the Vietnam Conflict," 236.

16. Chen, "China's Involvement," 379. At points, Beijing actually took supplies away from their own army to give them to Hanoi. Xiaoming, "Vietnam War," 737.

17. On the Vietminh use of Chinese sanctuaries in the French Indochina War see Fall, *Street Without Joy*, passim; Bernard B. Fall, *Hell in a Very Small Place: The Siege of Dien Bien Phu* (New York: De Capo Press, 1966), passim; Ronald H. Spector, *Advice and Support: The Early Years, 1941-1960* (Washington, DC: Center of Military History, 1983), 123-126; and Charles P. Biggio, "Let's Learn From the French," *Military Review*, 46 (October 1966), 33-34.

18. John Prados, *The Blood Road: The Ho Chi Minh Trail and the Vietnam War* (New York: John Wiley and Sons, 1999), 9-86, 373-374; Norman B. Hannah, *The Key to Failure: Laos and the Vietnam War* (Lanham, MD: Madison Books,

1987); John M. Shaw, *The Cambodian Campaign: The 1970 Offensive and America's Vietnam War* (Lawrence: University Press of Kansas, 2005), 5-10; Gregory T. Banner, "The War for the Ho Chi Minh Trail," Master's Thesis, US Army Command and General Staff College, 1993, 9-25; John T. Correll, "The Ho Chi Minh Trail," *Air Force Magazine*, 88 (November 2005), 62-68; Michael Lee Lanning and Dan Cragg, *Inside the VC and the NVA* (New York: Ivy Books, 1992), 74-156; Douglas Pike, *PAVN: People's Army of Vietnam* (Novato, CA: Presidio Press, 1986), 42-49; Richard L. Stevens, "A History of the Ho Chi Minh Trail and the Role of Nature in the War in Viet Nam," Ph.D. dissertation, (University of Hawaii, 1990), 5-180; Truong Nhu Tang, *A Vietcong Memoir* (San Diego, CA: Harcourt Brace Jovanovich, 1985), 127-129, 169; Christian G. Appy, *Patriots: The Vietnam War Remembered from All Sides* (New York: Viking, 2003), 101-106. An early description of the trail can be found in Edgar O'Ballance, "The Ho Chi Minh Trail," *Army Quarterly and Defense Journal*, 94 (April 1967), 105-110. It should be noted that COSVN did not require a massive structural headquarters. See Appy, *Patriots*, 382-383.

19. Quoted in Prados, *Blood Road*, 18-19. A particularly clear statement of the problem came from Colonel Edwin F. Black in 1965, "Advisory Warfare vs. Sanctuary Warfare," *U.S. Naval Institute Proceedings*, 91 (February 1965), 34-42.

20. Prados, *Blood Road*, 19.

21. Averell Harriman quoted in Michael E. Haas, *Apollo's Warriors: United States Air Force Special Operations during the Cold War* (Maxwell Air Force Base, AL: Air University Press, 1997), 175.

22. Shortly after the Geneva Accords, President John F. Kennedy met with several key advisers who informed him that the Vietnamese communists had no intention of withdrawing their troops. "Meeting on Laos," 28 September 1962, in Timothy Naftali and Philip Zelikow, eds., *The Presidential Recordings: John F. Kennedy, The Great Crises, Volume Two* (New York: W.W. Norton, 2001), 178-181. Americans and their allies would continue to gather information on North Vietnamese violations of Laotian neutrality. See United States Intelligence Board, "North Vietnamese Violations of the Geneva Agreements on Laos," 24 June 1964, Virtual Vietnam Archive, accessed 9 March 2006, and the Laotian "White Book on the Violations of the Geneva Accords of 1962 by the Government of North Vietnam," 1968, Virtual Vietnam Archive, accessed 9 March 2005.

23. Background on Army Special Forces can be found in Charles M. Simpson, *Inside the Green Berets: The First Thirty Years* (Novato, CA: Presidio Press, 1983), 11-75; Richard H. Shultz, *The Secret War Against Hanoi: Kennedy's and Johnson's Use of Spies, Saboteurs, and Covert Warriors in North Vietnam* (New York: HarperCollins, 1999), 1-8; and Francis J. Kelly, *U.S. Army Special Forces*,

41

Vietnam Studies, (Washington, DC: Center of Military History, 1973), 3-18. Useful information on Taylor and Kennedy is in Maxwell D. Taylor, *Swords and Plowshares* (New York: W.W. Norton, 1972); John M. Taylor, *General Maxwell Taylor: The Sword and the Pen* (New York: Doubleday, 1989), 192-258; Douglas Kinnard, *The Certain Trumpet: Maxwell Taylor and the American Experience in Vietnam* (Washington, DC: Brassey's, 1991).

24. For details see Kenneth Conboy, *Shadow War: The CIA's Secret War in Laos* (Boulder, CO: Paladin Press, 1995), 1-114; Shelby L. Stanton, *Green Berets at War: U.S. Army Special Forces in Southeast Asia, 1956-1975* (Novato, CA: Presidio Press, 1985), 16-43; Simpson, *Inside the Green Berets*, 87-94; and Shultz, *Secret War*, 13-15.

25. "Outline History of the 5th SF Gp, Participation in the CIDG Program, 1961-1970," Virtual Vietnam Archive, accessed 6 March 2006; Jeffrey J. Clarke, *Advice and Support: The Final Years, 1965-1973* (Washington, DC: Center of Military History, 1988), 69-74; Stanton, *Green Berets*, 35-86; and Kelly, *U.S. Army Special Forces*, 19-53, 182-193.

26. Secretary of Defense Robert McNamara called these operations "remarkably effective." See Kenneth Conboy, *Shadow War: The CIA's Secret War in Laos* (Boulder, CO: Paladin Press, 1995), 115-119. The CIA gave up most of its role in the border security issue in November 1963. Stanton, *Green Berets*, 65.

27. William Rosenau, *Special Operations Forces and Elusive Enemy Ground Targets: Lessons from Vietnam and the Persian Gulf War* (Santa Monica, CA: RAND, 2001), 8-10; and John L. Plaster, *SOG: The Secret Wars of America's Commandos in Vietnam* (New York: Simon and Schuster, 1997), 27-28.

28. SOG also took over the CIA's role in such operations. Plaster, *SOG*, 22-28; Shultz, *Secret War*, 31-49.

29. Rosenau, *Special Operations*, 18-19.

30. Shultz, *Secret War*, 65-68; Plaster, *SOG*, 34; Rosenau, *Special Operations*, 17-19; Clarke, *Final Years*, 195-207; and Robert L. Turkoly-Joczik, "Secrecy and Stealth: Cross-Border Reconnaissance in Indochina," *Military Intelligence Professional Bulletin*, 25 (July-September 1999), 47-52.

31. For a journalistic account of the life of forward air controllers flying over Laos, see Christopher Robbins, *The Ravens: The Men Who Flew in America's Secret War in Laos* (New York: Crown Publishers, 1987).

32. Shultz, *Secret War*, 204-257; Conboy, *Shadow War*, 377-378; Prados, *Blood Road*, passim; Plaster, *SOG*, passim; and Rosenau, *Special Operations*, 17-24.

33. John Crerar quoted in Rosenau, *Special Operations*, 25.

34. Ibid., 22.

35. Henry G. Gole, "Shadow Wars and Secret Wars: Phoenix and MACV-SOG," *Parameters*, 21 (Winter 1991-92), 104-105.

36. As one historian has argued, most American airpower advocates "assumed that in terms of airpower, protracted revolutionary warfare was just conventional warfare writ small." Dennis M. Drew, "U.S. Airpower Theory and the Insurgent Challenge: A Short Journey to Confusion," *Journal of Military History*, 62 (October 1998), 815. See also Earl H. Tilford, *Crosswinds: The Air Force's Setup in Vietnam* (College Station, TX: Texas A&M University Press, 1993), 3-64; William M. Momyer, *Airpower in Three Wars* (Maxwell Air Force Base, AL: Air University Press, 2003); and Mark Clodfelter, *The Limits of Airpower: The American Bombing of North Vietnam* (New York: Free Press, 1989), 1-44.

37. Jacob Van Staaveren, *Interdiction in Southern Laos, 1960-1968* (Washington, DC: Center for Air Force History, 1993), 23-44.

38. Ibid., 61.

39. Ibid., 107-253. The B-26K was redesignated as the A-26 because US Air Force bombers could not fly out of Thailand. No changes were made to the plane. See also Momyer, *Airpower*, 193-235, and Jack S. Ballard, *Development and Employment of Fixed Wing Gunships, 1962-1972* (Washington, DC: Office of Air Force History, 1982), 28-76.

40. Westmoreland, *Soldier Reports*, 196.

41. Statistics drawn from the appendices in Van Staaveren, *Interdiction*, 297-301.

42. O'Ballance, "Ho Chi Minh Trail," 109.

43. John Prados and Ray William Stubbe, *Valley of Decision: The Siege of Khe Sanh* (Boston: Houghton Mifflin, 1991); Bernard C. Nalty, *Airpower and the Fight for Khe Sanh* (Washington, DC: Office of Air Force History, 1986); Robert L. Pisor, *The End of the Line: The Siege of Khe Sanh* (New York: Norton, 1982).

44. Ronald H. Spector, *After Tet: The Bloodiest Year in Vietnam* (New York: Free Press, 1993), 1-25; Herring, *America's Longest War*, 203-228; Don Oberdorfer, *Tet!* (Garden City, NY: Doubleday, 1971); Marc Jason Gilbert and William Head, eds., *The Tet Offensive* (Westport, CT: Praeger, 1996).

45. For example, the US Army issued a field manual (FM) on denial barriers in 1968 and one on border security and anti-infiltration in 1972, and both had been influenced by the French experience and the difficulties of maintaining the DMZ in Korea. See Daniel P. Bolger, *Scenes from an Unfinished War: Low-Intensity Conflict in Korea, 1966-1969*, Leavenworth Paper No. 19, (Fort Leavenworth, KS: Combat Studies Institute Press, 1991), 44-47; US Department of the Army, FM 31-10, *Denial Operations and Barriers* (Washington, DC: GPO, September 1968); and US Department of the Army, FM 31-55, *Border Security/Anti-Infiltration Operations* (Washington, DC: GPO, March 1972).

46. Paul Dickson, *The Electronic Battlefield* (Bloomington: Indiana University Press, 1976), 20-52; Peter W. Brush, "The Story Behind the McNamara Line," *Vietnam* (February 1996), 18-24; George Weiss, "Battle for Control of the Ho

Chi Minh Trail," *Armed Forces Journal*, 108 (15 February 1971), 18-22; Van Staaveren, *Interdiction*, 255-283; Richard S. Greeley, "Stringing the McNamara Line," *Naval History*, 11 (July/August 1997), 60-61; and US Congress, Senate Armed Forces Committee, *Report of the Electronic Battlefield Program. 92d Congress, 1st Session* (Washington, DC: GPO, 1971), 1-8.

47. Brush, "The Story," 21.

48. Spector, *After Tet*, 222-231; Gary L. Telfer, et al., *U.S. Marines in Vietnam: Fighting the North Vietnamese, 1967* (Washington, DC: USMC History and Museums Division, 1984), 86-95, 227, 242.

49. *Report of the Electronic Battlefield*, 3-5; Dickson, *Electronic Battlefield*, passim; Weiss, "Battle for Control," 20-22; Van Staaveren, *Interdiction*, 267-283.

50. Bernard C. Nalty, *The War Against the Trucks: Aerial Interdiction in Southern Laos* (Washington, DC: Air Force History and Museums Program, 2005), passim; Herman J. Gilster, *The Air War in Southeast Asia: Case Studies of Selected Campaigns* (Maxwell Air Force Base, AL: Air University Press, 1993), 13-73; Momyer, *Airpower*, 237-276; Ballard, *Development of Fixed Wing Gunships*, 77-248; Tilford, *Crosswinds*, 108-118, 124-127; Shaw, *Cambodia Campaign*, 13-14.

51. Tilford, *Crosswinds*, xv, 109.

52. Shaw, *Cambodian Campaign*, 11-12.

53. Quoted in Prados, *Blood Road*, 102.

54. Spector, *After Tet*, 301. See also Dickson, *Electronic Battlefield*, 90-99.

55. Tang, *Vietcong Memoir*, 242.

56. Nalty, *War Against the Trucks*, 291-303; Tilford, *Crosswinds*, 114-116; Prados, *Blood Road*, passim; Banner, "War for the Ho Chi Minh Trail," 59-61; Appy, *Patriots*, 102.

57. Edward Lansdale, Harold K. Johnson, and John Paul Vann are just a few of the prominent individuals who wanted to focus on pacification first. See Office of the Deputy Chief of Staff for Military Operations, *A Program for the Pacification and Long-Term Development of South Vietnam*, 2 vols., (Department of the Army, 1966); Lewis Sorley, "To Change a War: General Harold K. Johnson and the PROVN Study," *Parameters*, 28 (Spring 1998), 93-109; Lewis Sorley, *Honorable Warrior: General Harold K. Johnson and the Ethics of Command* (Lawrence: University Press of Kansas, 1998); Neil Sheehan, *A Bright Shining Lie: John Paul Vann and America in Vietnam* (New York: Random House, 1988); and Cecil B. Currey, *Edward Lansdale: The Unquiet American* (Boston: Houghton Mifflin, 1988), 259-282.

58. Prados, *Blood Road*, 21.

59. United States Mission in Vietnam, "Viet Cong Use of Terror," March 1967, Virtual Vietnam Archive, accessed 2 March 2006. See also Guenter Lewy,

America in Vietnam (New York: Oxford University Press, 1978), 272-279.

60. Karnow, *Vietnam*, 231-239, 255-258, 323-324; Lewy, *America in Vietnam*, passim; James M. Higgins, "The Misapplication of the Malayan Counterinsurgency Model to the Strategic Hamlet Program," Master's thesis, US Army Command and General Staff College, 2001.

61. There is some debate as to the extent and permanence of the damage to the Vietcong, but most observers agree that the battles of 1968 negatively affected the insurgency, especially until the American withdrawal in 1973. NVA officer Bui Tin said in an interview in 1995 that "our forces in the South were nearly wiped out by all the fighting in 1968." "How North Vietnam Won the War," *Wall Street Journal* (3 August 1995), A8. See also Spector, *After Tet*, 310-316; Gates, "People's War," 336-344; Peter Brush, "The Significance of Local Communist Forces In Post-Tet Vietnam," online at http://www.library.vanderbilt.edu/central/brush/LocalForces.htm, accessed 27 February 2006; Lewis Sorley, *A Better War: The Unexamined Victories and Final Tragedy of America's Last Years in Vietnam* (New York: Harcourt Brace, 1999), 12-15.

62. Pacification included a variety of programs, including the Army's Civil Operations, Revolutionary Development Support (CORDS), the Marine's Combined Action Program (CAP), the Accelerated Pacification Program, and the PHOENIX program for eliminating Vietcong leadership. The literature on this aspect of the war is developing. See Sorley, *Better War*, passim; Lewis Sorley, ed., *Vietnam Chronicles: The Abrams Tapes, 1968-1972* (Lubbock, TX: Texas Tech University Press, 2004); James H. Willbanks, *Abandoning Vietnam: How America Left and South Vietnam Lost Its War* (Lawrence: University Press of Kansas, 2004), 5-58, 87-93; Richard A. Hunt, *Pacification: The American Struggle for Vietnam's Hearts and Minds* (Boulder, CO: Westview Press, 1995); Harry G. Summers, *On Strategy: The Vietnam War in Context* (Carlisle Barracks, PA: Strategic Studies Institute, 1982); Richard J. Macak, "The CORDS Pacification Program: An Operational Level Campaign Plan in Low Intensity Conflict," SAMS Monograph, (Fort Leavenworth, KS, May 1989); Clarke, *Final Years*, passim; Thomas W. Scoville, *Reorganizing for Pacification Support* (Washington, DC: Center of Military History, 1982); Tran Dinh Tho, *Pacification* (Washington, DC: Center of Military History, 1980); Keith F. Kopets, "The Combined Action Program: Vietnam," *Military Review*, 82 (July-August 2002), 78-81; Robert W. Komer, *Impact of Pacification on Insurgency in South Vietnam* (Santa Monica, CA: RAND, 1970); Frank L. Jones, "Blowtorch: Robert Komer and the Making of Vietnam Pacification Policy," *Parameters*, 35 (Autumn 2005), 103-118; Erwin R. Brigham, "Pacification Measurement," *Military Review*, 50 (May 1970), 47-55; Cassidy, "Back to the Street," 73-83; Timothy J. Lomperis, "Giap's Dream, Westmoreland's Nightmare," *Parameters*, 18 (June 1988), 18-32; Edward P. Metzner, *More Than a Soldier's War: Pacification*

in Vietnam (College Station, TX: Texas A&M University Press, 1995); Dale Andrade, *Ashes to Ashes: The Phoenix Program and the Vietnam War* (Lexington, MA: Lexington Books, 1990); Mark Moyar, *Phoenix and the Birds of Prey: The CIA's Secret Campaign to Destroy the Viet Cong* (Annapolis, MD: Naval Institute Press, 1997).

63. There is some debate about the degree of success and the damage done to the Vietcong in these years. See, for example, Krepinevich, *Army in Vietnam*, 254-257, and Lewy, *America in Vietnam*, passim. Most of the studies cited in the previous note argue that pacification was working to one degree or another. Even some skeptics have noted the decline in southern support for the Vietcong after 1968, including Stanley Karnow, *Vietnam*, 601-603, and Frances FitzGerald, *Fire in the Lake: The Vietnamese and Americans in Vietnam* (New York: Random House, 1983), 527. See also Davidson *Vietnam at War*, 633-635.

64. Shaw, *Cambodian Campaign*, 20-24.

65. The continued attacks compelled one Army officer to revive the idea of a barrier, only this time the line would extend along the entire border. George M. Shuffer, "An Appropriate Response," *Military Review*, 49 (December 1969), 91-96.

66. For example see Charles F. Brower, "Strategic Reassessment in Vietnam: The Westmoreland 'Alternate Strategy' of 1967-1968," *Naval War College Review*, 44 (Spring 1991), 20-51. A contemporary statement of the problem was Stefan T. Possony, "Battle, No Longer the Payoff?" *U.S. Naval Institute Proceedings*, 96 (September 1970), 33-37.

67. For the background on the campaign and Nixon's decision, including discussions of smaller ARVN cross border missions in April 1970, see Shaw, *Cambodian Campaign*, 23-62; Keith W. Nolan, *Into Cambodia: Spring Campaign, Summer Offensive, 1970* (Novato, CA: Presidio Press, 1990), 3-82; J.D. Coleman, *Incursion: From America's Chokehold on the NVA Lifelines to the Sacking of the Cambodian Sanctuaries* (New York: St. Martin's Paperbacks, 1991), 1-220; Dale Andrade, "Crossing the Line: Assault Into Cambodia," *Military History Quarterly* 13 (Winter 2001), 22-23; Tran Dinh Tho, *The Cambodian Incursion* (Washington, DC: Center of Military History, 1980), 1-50.

68. The American vessels stopped at the 20-mile limit. Shaw, *Cambodian Campaign*, 145-148; Tho, *Cambodian Incursion*, 83-100.

69. Leaflets: "Communist Cadre and Soldiers in Cambodia #1" and "Where Is Your Sanctuary Now?" May 1970, Virtual Vietnam Archive, accessed 12 December 2005.

70. Shaw, *Cambodian Campaign*, 63-79.

71. Andrade, "Crossing the Line," 26.

72. Ibid., 26. A personal recollection of the incursion from a combat engineer is Michael V. Meadows, "Into the Lion's Den," *Vietnam*, (August 2005), 18-24.

73. Coleman, *Incursion*, 254-261; Nolan, *Into Cambodia*, 331-370; Plaster, *SOG*, 246-250.

74. Willbanks, *Abandoning Vietnam*, 67-86; Shaw, *Cambodian Campaign*, 105-131; Nolan, *Into Cambodia*, 275-298.

75. Sorley, *Better War*, 200-214; Shaw, *Cambodian Campaign*, 153-170; Tho, *Cambodian Incursion*, 171-175; Clarke, *Final Years*, 418-425.

76. American pilots, helicopter and fixed wing, went along. American ground troops were to keep the supply line to the ARVN open in South Vietnam, in Operation DEWEY CANYON II. A solid summary of American efforts can be found in Richard K. Kolb, "Hitting the Ho Chi Minh Trail," *VFW, Veterans of Foreign Wars Magazine*, 83 (February 1996), 33-38. More detailed accounts of the background and American role are Keith W. Nolan, *Into Laos: the Story of Dewey Canyon II/Lam Son 719; Vietnam 1971* (Novato, CA: Presidio Press, 1986); Graham A. Cosmas and Terrence P. Murray, *U.S. Marines in Vietnam: Vietnamization and Redeployment, 1970-1971* (Washington, DC: USMC History and Museums Division, 1986), 195-210; Jim E. Fulbrook, "Lam Son 719: Part I: Prelude to Air Assault," *U.S. Army Aviation Digest*, 32 (June 1986), 2-15; Clarke, *Final Years*, 472-476.

77. Nguyen Duy Hinh, *Lam Son 719* (Washington, DC: Center of Military History, 1979); Jim E. Fulbrook, "Lam Son 719: Part II: The Battle," *U.S. Army Aviation Digest*, 32 (July 1986), 34-45; Willbanks, *Abandoning Vietnam*, 94-121; Nolan, *Into Laos*, 103-155, 259-356; Sorley, *Better War*, 243-260; Nalty, *War Against Trucks*, 151-156.

78. Cosmas and Murray, *Vietnamization*, 209-210; Nolan, *Into Laos*, 357-363; Sorley, *Better War*, 261-271; Sorley, ed., *Abrams Tapes*, 542-608; Jim E. Fulbrook, "Lam Son 719: Part III: Reflections and Values," *U.S. Army Aviation Digest*, 32 (August 1986), 3-13.

79. Hannah, *Key to Failure*, 277-296.

80. In April 1972, ARVN General Cao Van Vien acknowledged the progress being made in the counterinsurgency, and made yet another call for a barrier system along the Laotian and Cambodian borders. "Vietnam: What Next?" *Military Review*, 52 (April 1972), 22-30.

81. Chen, "China's Involvement," 379; Xiaoming, "Vietnam War," 738-739.

82. Quoted in Lewis Sorley, "Courage and Blood: South Vietnam's Repulse of the 1972 Easter Invasion," *Parameters*, 29 (Summer 1999), 40.

83. Dale Andrade, *America's Last Vietnam Battle: Halting Hanoi's 1972 Easter Offensive* (Lawrence: University Press of Kansas, 2001); Ngo Quang Truong, *The Easter Offensive of 1972* (Washington, DC: US Army Center of Military History, 1980); Willbanks, *Abandoning Vietnam*, 122-162; James H. Willbanks, *The Battle of An Loc* (Bloomington: University of Indiana Press, 2005); James H. Willbanks, *Thiet Giap! The Battle of An Loc* (Fort Leavenworth, KS: Combat

Studies Institute Press, 1993) 1-71; A.J. C. Lavalle, ed., *Airpower and the 1972 Spring Invasion* (Washington, DC: Office of Air Force History, 1985); Clarke, *Final Years*, 481-490; Sorley, "Courage and Blood," 38-56; Sorley, *Better War*, 318-342; Lam Quang Thi, *The Twenty-Five Year Century: A South Vietnamese General Remembers the Indochina War to the Fall of Saigon* (Denton, TX: University of North Texas Press, 2001), 263-290.

84. William E. Le Gro, *Vietnam from Cease-Fire to Capitulation* (Washington, DC: US Army Center of Military History, 1985); Willbanks, *Abandoning Vietnam*, 163-276; Davidson, *Vietnam at War*, 705-794; Karnow, *Vietnam*, 650-670; Appy, *Patriots*, 461-469, 493-507; Thi, *Twenty-Five Year Century*, 291-398.

85. "How North Vietnam Won," A8.

Chapter 2
Soviet–Afghan War

Shock

The presidential family spent Christmas 1979 alone at Camp David, waking up early to exchange gifts. Even at the holidays, even at the site of his greatest diplomatic triumph the year before, events weighed heavy on Jimmy Carter's mind. The Iranian hostage crisis—doomed to last 444 days—had already gone on for an interminable six weeks. The White House Christmas tree, a staple of the joyous season, had been left unlit in solidarity with the sixty-six Americans detained by Iranian radicals. Budget disputes awaited the president's return after the holidays. And to top it off, 1980 was an presidential election year, and Carter had to begin the arduous campaign to retain the White House.[1] Those dark days were about to get darker.

He was still at Camp David when the word came in two days later: the Soviet Union had invaded Afghanistan. Alarmed, President Carter flew to the White House.[2] That the Soviets had acted in Afghanistan was not a complete shock. The Soviets had been playing a significant role in Afghan affairs for years, and all during 1979 there were signs that they were about to step up their efforts. The shock came from the scale of the move.[3] As Carter later wrote, "In the past, Soviet leaders had not hesitated to use their own troops to maintain domination over the Warsaw Pact countries, or surrogate troops from Cuba and Vietnam to accomplish their ends elsewhere. However, this was the first time that they had used their troops to expand their sphere of influence since they had overthrown the government of Czechoslovakia in February 1948...."[4]

In the midst of a presidency that was trying to forge peace and healing after the upheavals of Vietnam and Watergate, the Soviet invasion of Afghanistan was an unwelcome turn of events, to say the least. It would not go unanswered. In responding, the United States would get to see the other side of the transnational sanctuary issue. The whole world would find out just how effective untouchable refuges and supply lines could be.

Background

There is nothing particularly inviting about Afghanistan. It is a moderate size country—slightly smaller than the state of Texas—covered with high mountains in the east and desert plains in the west. It has hot summers and cold winters, shortages of fresh water, and horrible earthquakes.[5] It is divided demographically. Ethnically, Afghanistan's 16 million people are a mix of Pashtuns in the south, Tajiks and Uzbeks in the north, and Hazara in the central mountains, and various others scattered throughout the country. These people speak a variety of languages, including Pashtu, Persian, and various Turkic languages, among many others. The country is primarily Sunni Muslim, but with a solid Shia minority.

Afghanistan may not seem inviting, but location is everything. Afghanistan sits at the crossroads of central Asia, a meeting point of Middle Eastern, South Asian, East Asian, and Eurasian cultures. And so it has been a key trade and invasion route for countless world empires, from the Persians and Alexander the Great in antiquity through the Mongols in the middle ages to the British in modern times.[6]

In the 20th century the newest empire to look toward Afghanistan and see opportunity was the communist Union of Soviet Socialist Republics. Afghanistan sat just to the south of the Soviet Union, along the borders of the Soviet republics of Turkmenistan, Uzbekistan, and Tajikistan, a buffer state between Russian territory and the British empire in India. In the 1920s the Soviets chased Muslim resistance fighters across the Afghan frontier as part of an effort to stabilize the border. It worked—Afghanistan remained neutral, even during World War II. After the war the communist strategy became more aggressive in the underdeveloped world, and the instability left by the partition of India in 1947 quickly brought Afghanistan back to the attention of Moscow. By the 1970s the Soviets had given the government of Afghanistan over $2 billion in military and economic aid in an effort to influence Afghan affairs.

The 1970s saw more upheaval than usual in Afghanistan, as a 1973 coup removed the royal family and set up a nominal republic. In 1978 another rebellion installed a communist regime in the capital of Kabul. But the communists fought among themselves, a series of rebellions began, the national military started to disintegrate, and violence broke out all over the country. To try to bring some stability to this state of affairs, in September 1979 the Soviets helped a man named Hafizullah Amin take power in Afghanistan. Yet the situation continued to deteriorate.

MAP 3. SANCTUARIES ON THE AFGHANISTAN / PAKISTAN BORDER.

By this time Moscow developed greater interest in their southern neighbor. It helped that Afghanistan was the path south and west, the route toward both the oil rich Middle East and the long-coveted warm water port on the Indian Ocean. Also, the geopolitical situation invited action. The United States, the Soviet Union's great power rival, had just concluded its costly war in Vietnam. American presidents Richard Nixon, Gerald Ford, and Jimmy Carter had for the better part of the decade pursued the conciliatory policy of détente toward the USSR. Recent Soviet actions elsewhere in the developing world, for example Angola, had been met with indifference by the free world. And in 1979, the Iranian revolution and hostage crisis consumed much of America's attention. With Afghanistan in chaos, the time for Soviet intervention was at hand.

The Soviets already had thousands of advisors in country, but for much of the fall of 1979 they prepared to increase drastically their presence in Afghanistan. The process accelerated in late November and early December, as the Russians brought troops to the borders. On Christmas Eve and Christmas Day, the invasion began in earnest, as the Soviets crossed the border and airlifted a large force into Kabul International Airport. On 27 December KGB commandos led an assault on the presidential palace. Amin, the man who had allegedly invited the Soviet intervention, died in the attack. Babrak Kamal, Amin's communist rival, became the new president. In the next few months, roughly 85,000 Soviet troops entered Afghanistan; by 1982 the number was nearly 115,000, where it would stay for most of the rest of the war.[7]

Before the Soviets ever intervened, Afghanistan had descended into near-anarchy, with competing factions of all different stripes fighting it out for power, independence, and political and religious rights. The Soviet Union's intervention made the Soviets directly responsible for bringing order to this chaos—they no longer could rely on aid to puppet leaders to keep Afghanistan stable and friendly. The intervention had another effect, with results that would take years to see. The hopelessly fractured regional, ethnic, and religious strands within the political body known as Afghanistan now had a common enemy—for the first time in a long time, the people of Afghanistan potentially had a reason to work together on something. But they could not do it on their own.

The Resistances and Their Friends

The communists ran into trouble right away. The Soviets and the Kabul government enforced radical reforms that challenged local traditions.[8] The people of Afghanistan resented such coercion and reacted immediately. The various factions that had already been fighting throughout the country kept right on fighting, only many of them turned their efforts against the Russian troops. The Afghan army fell apart and thousands deserted. Conditions became so bad under Soviet control during this multiparty civil war that millions of Afghans fled the country. Refugees flooded into neighboring Pakistan and Iran, creating a humanitarian crisis in the border areas. The international community had to find a way to work with the Pakistanis and Iranians to prevent the deaths of millions.[9]

To make matters even more confusing, there was no unity among the various anti-Soviet parties. In fact, it would be more precise to refer to multiple resistances against the Soviet regime, each driven by their own motivations. The individual groups came to be known collectively as the Mujahideen, but they divided along regional, ethnic, and religious lines into small groups to fight the Russians.[10] Numbering at least in the hundreds, but more likely in the thousands, these smaller groups came under the leadership of local warlords or semi-independent commanders. Most of these groups had some connection with one of at least seven resistance parties, each based outside of Afghanistan. However, the parties never worked together in any real way and never provided any sort of coherent and unified strategy for the resistance groups.[11]

By and large, the Mujahideen fought in small units of anywhere between 80 and 150 men, and each group followed its own course of action. There were some more developed and sizable resistance organizations. In the west, Ismael Khan led a large force of as many as 5,000 in Herat.[12] But most of the larger resistance groups operated in the southern and eastern portions of Afghanistan. The most popular single figure among the resistance within Afghanistan was Ahmad Shah Massoud, an ethnic Tajik from the Panjshir valley, northeast of Kabul. At times during the Soviet-Afghan War, the so-called "Lion of Panjshir" commanded thousands of troops. His efforts consumed a great deal of Soviet attention throughout the fighting.[13]

In some regions the resistance groups came under the influence of radical Islam. Shia fundamentalists, inspired by the Iranian revolution, made up one such group, but they remained relatively small. The Sunnis broke into even more factions, including fundamentalists and radical Islamists, and some of whom worked with other resistance groups. Abdurrab Rasul Sayyaf led another radical Sunni wing of the resistance, including some Wahhabis. This religious aspect of the Mujahideen meant that during the war Afghanistan became a magnet for the most radical true believers of the Muslim world. Devout outsiders flooded into the country, inspired by the chance to engage in a holy struggle against the atheistic, communist Soviets.[14]

These Mujahideen shared a common enemy but never worked together in any meaningful way. However, for all their differences, many of these groups did have two vital things in common: the support of the wider world, and access to safe sanctuary and relatively easy supply across an international border. The international community almost as a whole condemned the Soviet invasion, and a few countries were prepared to offer direct aid to the resistances.[15] Saudi Arabia gave monetary and some material assistance to some of the fighters, especially the radical Muslim groups led by Sayyaf. Acting independent of other powers, Saudi intelligence funneled huge amounts of money in the form of gold, cash, and checks to these Mujahideen, which they used to fund their war.[16] Egypt also played a role, giving Soviet-made weapons to the resistance and even going so far as to train Afghan resistance fighters on Egyptian territory.[17] Saudi and Egyptian assistance played a key role in sustaining the Mujahideen.

The most comprehensive outside contribution to the resistance came from the Soviet Union's great power rival, the United States. Even before the Soviet invasion, the CIA had been active on a small scale in the internecine fighting in Afghanistan. The Iranian revolution had destabilized the region, and the Americans did not want to see the Soviets take advantage of that instability to gain direct access to the Middle East and Indian Ocean. Earlier in 1979, President Carter approved a half million dollars for the CIA to spend in Afghanistan on propaganda, radio equipment, and medical supplies for some of the rebel groups.[18] This increased focus on the region only grew after the December coup.

President Carter took the invasion personally and acted decisively, especially considering his more restrained responses to earlier crises. Soviet actions triggered the announcement of the so-called Carter Doctrine, in which the president declared that "An attempt by any outside force to gain control of the Persian Gulf region will be regarded as an assault on the vital interests of the United States of America, and such an assault will be repelled by any means necessary, including military force."[19] Within days of the Soviet invasion, National Security Advisor Zbigniew Brzezinski laid out the basic American strategy for the war in Afghanistan: "It is essential that Afghanistan's resistance continues. This means more money as well as arms shipments to the rebels, and some technical advice."[20]

When it came to aiding the resistances, the Carter administration was as good as its word. One week after the invasion, the Americans began purchasing Soviet-made weapons from the Egyptians to give to the Mujahideen. Egyptian president Anwar Sadat later said, "The United States sent me airplanes and told me, please open your stores for us so that we can give the Afghans the armaments they need to fight, and I gave the armaments."[21] Likewise, the CIA bought thousands of .303 Lee Enfield rifles and RPG-7 rocket propelled grenade launchers from around the world to send to the guerillas. A careful student of the CIA effort in those early years described the Agency's conception of its strategy in blunt terms: "to supply hundreds of thousands of rifles and tens of millions of bullets en masse to the guerillas and then sit back … and watch."[22]

For all the American enthusiasm about the opportunity to make the Soviets pay for their aggression, Brzezinski worried about the inherent weaknesses of the Mujahideen. He did not think they had much of a chance to expel the Soviets, and he explicitly compared the situation in Afghanistan in those early days of the rebellion to America's war in Vietnam:

> The guerillas are badly organized and poorly led. *They have no sanctuary*, no organized army, and no central government – all of which North Vietnam had. They have limited foreign support, in contrast to the enormous amount of arms that flowed to the Vietnamese from both the Soviet Union and China. The Soviets are likely to act decisively, unlike the U.S. ... in Vietnam....[23]

Brzezinski's point was clear: the guerrillas needed assistance, and in order for all of this outside aid to make a difference, it needed some way to get into Afghanistan.

The Borders

Afghanistan's centralized location meant that it had long borders with multiple countries, which offered several opportunities to find transnational sanctuaries and supply lines. The question was which country would be most important. For obvious reasons they could not use the three Soviet republics. That left Iran, China, and Pakistan.

Iran's 550-mile shared border with Afghanistan made it impossible for the Iranians to stay out of the war entirely. Hundreds of thousands of Afghan refugees fled west into Iran at the start of the conflict. At several times during the fight, the Soviets chased resistance fighters to the western border, where the Mujahideen crossed over for protection. The revolutionary Iranians also felt some camaraderie toward the resistance, especially the more radical Shia Islamic groups. As a result Iran offered open sympathy, limited aid, training, and occasionally refuge to the Mujahideen fighting in western Afghanistan.

Still, the Iranian role in the war remained limited, in part because the rebels did not focus the majority of their efforts in western Afghanistan where the open terrain made it more difficult to find shelter, but also because in 1980 Saddam Hussein's Iraqi forces invaded Iranian territory. The long eight-year bloodletting known as the Iran-Iraq War held most of Iran's attention during the Soviet-Afghan War. At the same time, the Iranians had limited resources, and the ayatollahs' hostility toward the United

States precluded even an alliance of convenience with the majority resistance groups.[24] Additionally, Soviet forays into Iran and diplomatic pressure on the ayatollahs convinced the Iranians to severely curtail resistance activities on their border.[25]

Another country that barely bordered Afghanistan played a larger role in opposing the Soviet occupation. A small spit of land juts out from northeastern corner of Afghanistan, a corridor appended to the country by the British in the 19th century to ensure that no portion of Russian territory came into contact with India. The so-called Wakhan corridor served its purpose well, but had the side effect of connecting Afghanistan to China. This shared border, though less than 50 miles in length and through some of the highest country on earth, gave China a physical and psychological bond with Afghanistan. The Chinese, who had already been feuding with the Soviets for nearly 15 years, feared that the takeover of Afghanistan would further weaken their strategic situation vis-à-vis their erstwhile communist allies. Put simply, the Chinese did not want to be surrounded by the Soviets and Soviet proxies. As a result, Chinese leadership made public pronouncements opposing the Soviet occupation and demanding withdrawal. More covertly, the Chinese gave the resistance aid in the form of small arms, rocket launchers, and heavy artillery.[26]

But that aid did not come across the short Chinese-Afghanistan border. The mountainous terrain and narrowness of the Wakhan corridor in the northeast made it easier for the Soviets to isolate. In the summer of 1980, "By establishing Soviet garrisons at the two main passes into China and Pakistan, occupying the entrance to the corridor from Afghanistan, improving the road to the Soviet frontier, and mining the passes from China and Pakistan to stop arms movements, the Soviet Union effectively cut the corridor off."[27] Chinese assistance to the Mujahideen, along with aid from everyone else, would have to come from elsewhere.

Only one option was left, as the Americans understood all too well. In the 1979 memo that described the weaknesses of the resistance, Brzezinski also explained that the United States had to "reassure Pakistan and encourage it to help the rebels…."[28] Pakistan, which shared a nearly 1,500-mile border with Afghanistan, needed reassurance and encouragement because it was in a precarious position. Much as they had with the Iranians, the Soviets explicitly threatened to invade Pakistan if it became involved in the war. And much like the Iranians, the Pakistanis had other concerns, most importantly, ongoing disputes with India. These concerns meant that Pakistan went to great lengths to avoid open aid to the resistances. But that caution did not make Pakistan neutral in the Soviet-Afghan War, far from it.

In addition to becoming the temporary home for the millions of Afghan refugees who fled the war, Pakistan played the most important role in facilitating the resistance. Refugees were not the only ones who fled over the border. Most of the exiled Afghan resistance parties went to Pakistan and directed their efforts within Afghanistan from across the border in Peshawar. The rugged terrain and harsh conditions along the winding and mountainous Afghanistan-Pakistan border was in many ways an ideal boundary over which to fight and aid an insurgency. Hundreds of mountain passes connected the two countries, the terrain made it impossible to close all these routes across the border, and the harsh conditions helped protect fleeing rebels. As a result, Pakistan became the primary sanctuary for the Mujahideen in Afghanistan. Not only that, it also became the essential supply route for the weapons and materiel that kept the Mujahideen going throughout the war. Pakistan became the funnel to the resistance for the outside world.[29]

The Pakistanis put several important conditions on the use of their territory. Throughout the early years of the war, the Pakistanis insisted that the Americans have no direct contact with the rebels. Everything had to be run through Pakistani intelligence. One observer described this process of providing arms to the rebels:

> First, the CIA bought weapons, using Saudi as well as American funds. The CIA transported the weapons to Pakistan, mostly by sea to the port of Karachi, but occasionally by air to Islamabad. Second, [Pakistani intelligence] took custody once the weapons had arrived in Pakistan. It transported the containers in much smaller quantities to warehouses near Rawalpindi ... or Quetta. It then trucked the weapons to depots controlled by the mujahidin groups in the border region.... Third, the parties distributed the weapons to commanders and oversaw their transport into Afghanistan by private entrepreneurs.[30]

The Americans agreed to all of this, and as a result, countless amounts of money and supplies got lost or stolen by middlemen in the chaotic and corrupt borderlands. Such was the price the United States was willing to pay to make use of such a prime sanctuary as Pakistan.[31]

One Pakistani official arriving on the frontier in 1983 remembered "The border areas of Pakistan had grown into a vast, sprawling administrative base for the [Jihad]. The Mujahideen came there for arms, they came to rest, they came to settle their families into camps, they came for training and they came for medical attention."[32] The relative ease and openness of early cross-border activities could be seen in journalist Edward Girardet's description of the infiltration routes (which he called the "Jihad Trail") and how those entrepreneurs made use of them:

> ...a significant amount of guerilla supplies, ranging from guns and ammunition to medicines, are brought in by horse, camel and mule trains across the more than 300 traditional caravan routes and goat tracks that lace the mountainous frontier between the two countries. With the rise of modern road traffic during the 1950s and 1960s, many of these caravan routes had fallen into disuse except by tribal nomads and smugglers. In the wake of the communist revolution, they rapidly reverted to their former use, except this time mainly by refugees and mujahideen.[33]

Teahouses sprung up along these routes, where, "For a small sum... the traveling mujahed can drink tea from streaming samovars and eat a meal, usually 'nan' dipped in a greasy meat and vegetable broth, before rolling up in his paout to sleep."[34]

It would not always be so easy or open.

Early Fighting, Early Adjustments

The resistance groups operated mostly outside the major cities. At first they used weapons they captured from the Soviets or that had been taken from the Afghan army by deserters, but as outside aid flooded in, they used newer and more complex weapons.[35] Their standard operations involved ambushing convoys between the population centers. They generally avoided attacks on established positions because of weakness in command and control and lack of skill in using indirect fire. An expert on the resistance described their common, low-tech tactics for attacking convoys:

> Ambushes involve one or two groups; most of the group members provide cover, while those who are carrying RPG-7 anti-tank rocket-launchers (rarely more than two on each operation) move forward until they are within a range of less than 100 m, for they rarely use sighting gear. The road has been mined in advance, and the attack is directed at the head of the convoy or at the rear. When the first vehicle has been blown up, each man carrying a rocket-launcher fires off one or two rockets and then withdraws. As soon as the forward unit

has rejoined the unit providing cover everyone withdraws in no particular order and without taking many precautions.[36]

These attacks were often successful in inflicting heavy casualties on the Soviet and Afghan troops, especially early on in the war, and much of the conflict evolved into a struggle over the major roads crisscrossing the country. Indeed, the Soviets never gained proper control of the vast majority of the countryside, but that did not mean that they did not adjust to the guerrilla threat.[37]

By the end of 1980, the Soviets had realized that tanks, armored vehicles, and large infantry units were cumbersome in fighting the resistance in the Afghan mountains, so they reorganized and switched tactics. "Consequently, the Soviets have increasingly deployed helicopter borne commandos, backed by columns of motorized infantry."[38] As the war went on, larger communist operations in Afghanistan often involved using helicopters to drop commandos behind enemy positions. Rapid motorized attacks would then drive the rebels into the commando positions.[39] Rebel leader Massoud commented on the effectiveness of the change in tactics, "It has become a very hard war, far harder than before. Their commandos have learned a great deal about mountain guerrilla warfare and are fighting much better than before."[40]

In addition, the Soviets stepped up their efforts to pacify the civilian villages in the countryside. They chose to ignore some areas. For example, the Hazara of the central mountains resisted the Soviets, but not as actively as other groups. They preferred remaining isolated and autonomous, and for much of the war they fought among themselves for control of the region. In any case, they did not have the logistical ability to keep up sustained operations against the Soviets.[41] The same held for the fighters in the northern provinces. As one wartime correspondent wrote, the Mujahideen in the north "suffered from their remoteness." It was "difficult for them to get arms in and news out."[42] In both areas the Soviets made some moves but were by and large content to allow the locals to remain isolated and out of the war.

In less isolated areas the Soviets tried other techniques. Rather than attempt to win over the locals by providing security and stability, the communists chose to try to eliminate potentially hostile civilians through force and fear. The Soviets began using all manner of weapons on the civilian population, including shelling and bombing unfriendly population centers. And in order to prevent supporters of the guerillas from returning to their homes, the Russians "deliberately wrecked irrigation systems, burned crops, killed livestock, and contaminated water sources...."[43] They dropped mines around villages and in livestock pastures and left explosive devices in food bins, fruit trees, disguised as toys, and even on dead bodies that would explode when families tried to recover them for burial. The villagers fled by the thousands from such destruction, joining the millions of other refugees from the war. Entire villages disappeared.[44]

Such techniques did not win the war for the communists, but they made it very difficult for more isolated resistance groups to feed and equip their troops from local sources. For example, as one analyst noted, to reach the Panjshir valley from Pakistan, "arms convoys of pack horses and donkeys...had to cross at least four mountain passes at an average altitude of 15,000 feet. For more distant resistance localities the trip to or from Pakistan could take a month."[45] So, for example, while the repeated Soviet pacification operations in the Panjshir valley did not defeat Massoud's force, they did force him to appeal for more outside aid and even to sign a short-lived cease-fire with the Soviets.[46] The communist savagery indicated a serious weakness in Soviet counterinsurgency doctrine and the Soviet frustration at not being able to put down the insurgency quickly.[47] But to the degree that it was successful at denying the guerrillas sanctuary within Afghanistan, it also made outside aid even more important to the rebel efforts, and everyone on both sides knew it.

Two experts on rebel tactics explained the changes brought about by the Soviet destruction of the agricultural system in Afghanistan:

> The Mujahideen factions responded to this crisis by establishing fixed supply bases within Afghanistan. The larger supply bases were located in the mountains near the Pakistan border. Small supply bases were caches hidden outside of towns and villages. The Soviets then concentrated on finding and destroying the large and small supply bases. The Mujahideen dependence on the large fixed supply bases meant that they had to defend them. This provided a viable target set for Soviet air and artillery.[48]

The proximity of the larger bases to the border and the difficulty of transport within Afghanistan served as further proof of the indispensable nature of the sanctuaries and supply lines in Pakistan to the Mujahideen.

The Soviets understood that they had a serious problem with the porous Pakistani border and the rebel sanctuaries within Pakistan, and they set out to find solutions, with varying degrees of success.[49] The communists tried a handful of approaches to deal with Pakistani sanctuary. The first and most consistent was the diplomatic attempt to threaten the Pakistanis into closing their own border. Throughout the war the communists made not-too-subtle hints that they would invade Pakistan if the Pakistanis continued to provide refuge for the guerillas. To support such threats, Soviet and Afghan airplanes and helicopters launched multiple air raids across the border to attack rebel bases and Afghan refugee camps. The Soviets and their Afghan allies also used artillery to shell across the border.

Such attacks did minor damage and killed hundreds of Afghans and Pakistanis a few at a time. The Pakistanis protested loudly, and drew in more support from the outside world by recounting the dead and warning of the Soviet threat. The attacks worked to the extent that Pakistan consistently and publicly disavowed any support for the Mujahideen. All the while, however, the Pakistanis allowed Pakistan's territory to be used as a refuge and Pakistani intelligence continued to work with foreign powers to fund and supply the Mujahideen.[50]

The Soviets also tried to use their intelligence agencies to threaten Pakistan and cut off resistance activities along the frontier. They bought off local tribal leaders along the border. For a while they even succeeded in raising some local militia units called Revolution Defense Groups to protect the border regions.[51] At times Soviet and Afghan intelligence succeeded in bribing poor villagers into launching sabotage missions in Afghan refugee camps and Pakistani towns. One Pakistani official explained, "Ever since the Russians came, they have paid huge sums to the tribals for sabotage, to make trouble.... The people are poor. If a poor man is offered 10,000 or 20,000 rupees, even if it is just 1 or 2 percent of the people, they can create a lot of trouble."[52] The trouble became an irritant to Pakistan, but did not change Pakistani policy toward providing the rebels sanctuary.

The most important and sustained effort from the Soviets to deny the Mujahideen their Pakistani sanctuary involved using military power to seal off the border. For example, for a while the Soviets contemplated building some sort of extended denial barrier along the frontier. In September 1982, an Afghan official announced that the communists had plans in place for a serious border security system, including guard towers, fences, and minefields. "If we do not reach an agreement with Pakistan soon," the official stated, "we have no other recourse but to close off lengthy sections of the frontier, however expensive that might turn out to be."[53] Obviously the communists intended this public threat to force the Pakistanis to act, but that did not mean that the Soviets lied about their plans to close the borders. An ex-KGB agent later reported that Soviet military command had a plan in place to seal the frontiers while airborne troops "would then simultaneously annihilate the partisan formations shut up in Afghanistan."[54] Unfortunately for the communists, such designs required at least 300,000 Russian troops along the border, far more than the Soviets were willing to commit.[55] In lieu of a proper barrier, the Soviets dropped thousands of mines on the border, especially along the important supply routes and mountain passes.[56]

As early as December 1981, they launched large scale military operations combining airpower and armored units to sweep through the frontier regions and cut off the supply routes. In 1984 and 1985, when the Soviets sent in more troops and stepped up their efforts along the border, the Mujahideen started to suffer.[57] The communists increased the frequency and intensity of air strikes and artillery bombardments of targets over the border. One journalist reported in November 1984 that the Pakistani border had been violated "several hundred times in the past three months."[58] In August 1985 the Soviets and crack troops from the Afghan army launched a two-pronged offensive at the Parrot's Beak, a section of the Afghanistan-Pakistan border that juts into Afghanistan pointing directly at Kabul and only 50 miles from the capital. The offensive cleared the area of Mujahideen.[59] One observer reported that in 1985 "Air attacks on resistance caravans became more frequent and precise.... Ambushes of mujahidin caravans by small units of [Soviet special forces] commandos positioned days in advance by helicopter also increased."[60] In the spring of 1986 another large communist operation consisting of Soviet and Afghan troops targeted Zhawar, the location of a rebel base on the border south of the communist base at Khost. The Mujahideen had held off a smaller attack the previous September, but this time the communists pounded the base into submission by the end of April.[61] Soviet airpower, especially helicopters as gunships and troop carriers, played a key role in these operations. These efforts were taking a serious toll on guerilla forces.

The situation clearly deteriorated for the Mujahideen as a result of the communist efforts along the border. The rebels who had once stopped at relatively comfortable teahouses on the paths into Afghanistan now found themselves forced to travel in darkness and silence. They no longer lit fires or ate hot food along the way.[62] In 1987, one observer wrote:

> By the spring of 1986, the Soviet forces in Afghanistan had
> achieved considerable military success against the Afghan

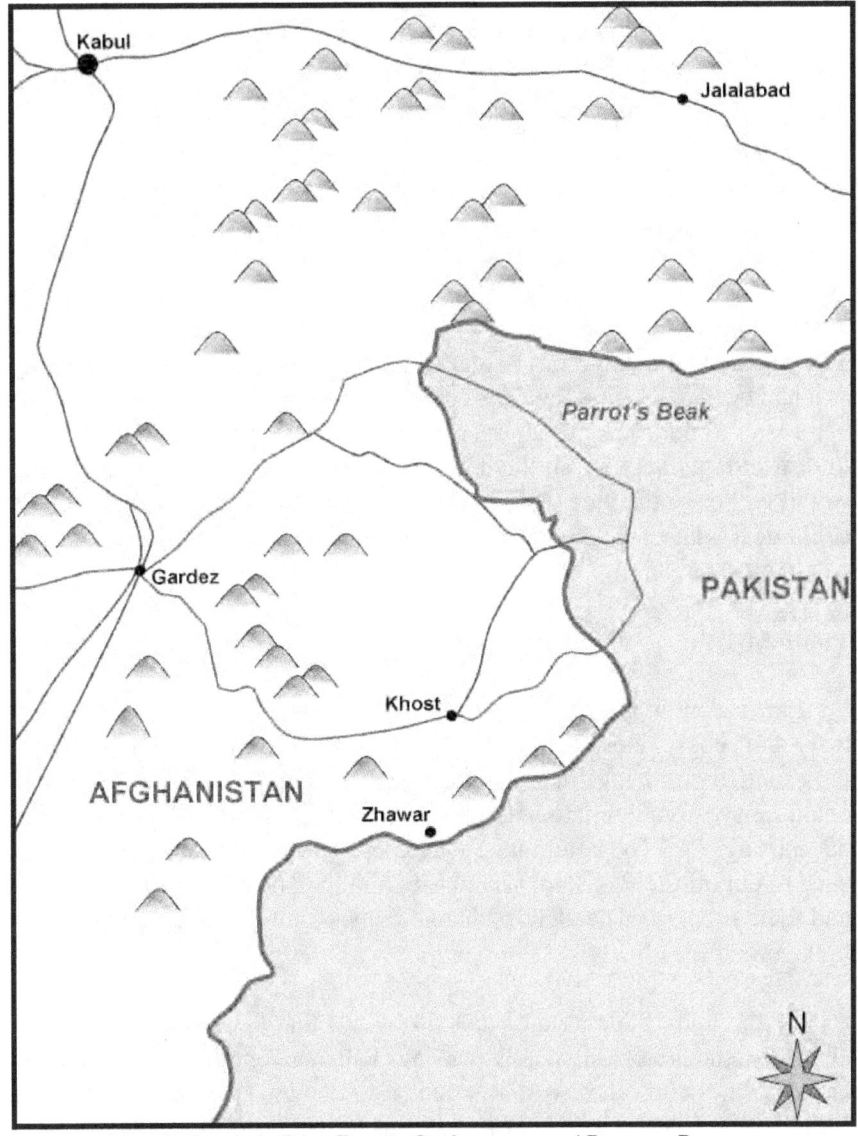

MAP 4. PARROT'S BEAK REGION ON AFGHANISTAN / PAKISTAN BORDER.

guerillas. Tactics included carpet bombing of agricultural regions and wholesale destruction of villages. The Soviets have created a 30-mile deep no-man's-land on the border with Pakistan. This has led to widespread food shortages and destroyed the guerillas' infrastructure in many regions. Soviet commando operations and air strikes against guerrilla caravans bringing in CIA-provided military supplies have forced some guerrilla units to abandon their bases and return to the refugee camps in Pakistan, from where they can only mount short hit-and-run raids into Afghanistan.[63]

In June 1986 the CIA agents on the ground in Pakistan had the impression that "sharply focused helicopter-borne special operations against resistance infiltration routes and strongholds had paid off for the Soviets. The war was going badly for the resistance."[64]

These descriptions probably exaggerated the depth of the problem for the rebels and the effectiveness of the Soviet border operations, but they did indicate that using cross border sanctuaries was nowhere near as easy as it had been in the first few years of the war. The communists had figured out a way to put their air superiority to good use. If they could continue to restrict rebel activity on the borders, the resistance within Afghanistan would wither on the vine. As one rebel commander said at the time, "If we could deal with their helicopter gunships, the whole spectrum of the war would change."65

Those Missiles

Experts on the region recognized the importance of keeping the sanctuary and supply lines open. In 1984 scholar Rosanne Klass wrote, "Without sanctuary and logistical support via Pakistan, the Afghan resistance could be swiftly decimated, as was the isolated Central Asian resistance 50 years ago."66 The communist successes of 1984 and early 1985 threatened to cut off the Pakistani sanctuaries and logistical support. The rebels and their supporters needed to change tactics, and the United States was in the mood to help.

By the mid-1980s it had become obvious that the Soviets were hesitant to extend an already costly war into Pakistan, let alone challenge the United States and other western countries for their fairly open aid to the Mujahideen. Consequently, the Americans felt more comfortable with giving more open aid to the resistance. In addition, President Ronald Reagan's administration took a more aggressive approach to fighting the Cold War.[67] Exact figures vary, but according to one source, "American aid started at about $30 million in 1980 [and] went up to about $50 million in 1981 and 1982. Under the Reagan administration this amount increased to $80 million in fiscal 1983 and $120 million in 1984."[68] The quality of the assistance increased along with the quantity. Beginning in January 1983, the CIA began delivering, for "the first time, some heavier weapons, including bazookas, mortars, grenade launchers, mines, and recoilless rifles...."[69]

Reagan had several strong allies in Congress in this effort, especially Texas Congressman Charles Wilson, who pushed for an even more aggressive US role in Afghanistan.[70] As a result of their efforts, the amount of monetary aid to the Mujahideen skyrocketed in the Reagan years, as did the quantity and variety of weapons sent to the rebels.[71] Congress doubled Reagan's 1985 request and gave $250 million for the Mujahideen. In 1986 the figure was $470 million; in 1987 it jumped to $630 million.[72] In March 1985, Reagan even signed a new National Security Decision Directive that gave American intelligence the more ambitious objective of not just harassing the Soviets, but giving the Mujahideen the means to drive the Soviets out of Afghanistan.[73]

A significant portion of this assistance aimed at keeping open and enhancing the links between the sanctuaries in Pakistan and the rebels in Afghanistan. Such efforts led to one of the more amusing aspects of American aid. In 1987 there was a shortage of mules for the guerillas in Afghanistan due to a local epidemic and Soviet mines. To help solve this problem, some newspapers reported that the CIA sent in mules from Missouri and Texas.[74] Apparently there were not enough American animals to meet the needs of the rebels, so according to one CIA official, the Agency began "importing thousands of Chinese mules into Afghanistan to transport weapons."[75] As absurd as it might sound to air transport pack animals across oceans or to import them from China, it was really an indication of the desperate need to keep open the mountain routes between Pakistan and Afghanistan.[76]

The main focus of the increased American aid to the Mujahideen in the Reagan years made even more apparent how much the Americans valued the infiltration routes, and how much the Soviet airpower worried them. In the spring of 1985, the CIA predicted that "the Soviets will place more emphasis on efforts to halt insurgent infiltration, mainly through greater use of airpower along Afghan borders with Pakistan...."[77] Fortunately for the rebels, the Americans had a countermeasure in mind.

From the beginning of the war the Chinese especially had provided antiaircraft machine guns to the Mujahideen. At points in the war, in sieges in towns along the border, the rebels had put these guns to good effect. But effective antiaircraft guns required organizational coherence, technical skill, and logistical expertise that most of the resistance groups just did not have. Likewise, the introduction of Soviet-made SA-7 surface to air missiles did not fundamentally challenge Soviet air power because of the weapon's inaccuracy and the development of effective communist countermeasures.[78] The Mujahideen required a simpler option, and the United States had a solution: handheld, accurate, and tactically viable antiaircraft missiles.

In 1985, the CIA and British intelligence began sending Blowpipe missiles to Afghanistan, and hundreds arrived in the first few months of 1986.[79] The Blowpipes were by then obsolete and had been replaced in the British military by updated systems, and they did not perform well for the Afghan rebels. A CIA official described the main problem with the Blowpipe: "the gunner had to acquire his target optically, fire the missile, and then stand his ground, usually upright and in the open, while he guided the missile with a toggle all the way to the target."[80] However, 1986 also saw the introduction of a far more effective antiaircraft weapon, the American-made FIM-92 Stinger missile.[81] The Stinger, by contrast with the Blowpipe, was a very accurate "fire and forget" missile. That meant that the Mujahideen could seek refuge after firing and live to fight another day. In next few years, the United States distributed to the rebel groups between 2,000 and 2,500 Stinger missiles.[82]

At the time, some experts feared that the missile would prove too complex for use by the resistance fighters. But as one writer at the time noted, "In practice, it turned out, the 18 steps needed to fire the weapon, while they require considerable practice and fast thinking, were not much more complex than the procedures used by footsoldiers of the Revolutionary War to load and fire their muskets."[83] To help with the process, American instructors at the camps within Pakistan gave direct guidance to the guerillas on the use of the missiles.[84] Besides, the guerillas may have had added incentive to learn quick; the Soviets learned that among some resistance groups, "failure to bring down at least one aircraft with three Stingers was punishable by death."[85]

The first documented use of the Stingers in Afghanistan happened on 25 September 1986 northeast of Jalalabad. There a team of Mujahideen fired four missiles and destroyed three Soviet helicopter gunships. The rebels filmed the attack, and the tape, along with a used tube from one of the missiles, eventually made its way to President Reagan. CIA Director William Casey became so enthusiastic about the successful mission that he felt certain that the Soviet effort in Afghanistan was doomed.[86] In the months and years that followed, communist aircraft losses shot up sharply, due in no small part to the Stinger. At the same time, Soviet and Afghan pilots became hesitant to fly at lower altitudes within range of the missiles.

The Mujahideen could once again operate more freely on the ground in Afghanistan and along the frontier.[87]

One expert on the war opined that the Mujahideen could keep supply roads open in part because "they could establish heavily protected strongholds in the mountains, because the Soviets, through fear of the Stingers, were relying more on artillery than on air power...." In addition, "Stingers and better weaponry also made it more costly for the Soviets to carry out routine operations, such as patrolling along supply roads or providing air support to besieged government outposts."[88] A CIA agent on the scene agreed, reporting in January 1987 that the majority of convoys made it through the border. According to the agent, credit belonged to the Stingers, the "most significant battlefield development during the last six months...."[89] Another report noted that missiles improved morale among the Mujahideen so much that they "were pouring into eastern Afghanistan, now that interdiction by Soviet and [Afghan] aircraft of their infiltration routes seemed reduced."[90]

The Stinger missile did not win the war on its own, but its introduction did factor into the success of the Mujahideen in the last years of the Soviet war and it did indicate just how important sanctuary was to the rebel war effort. For one thing, the guerrillas never could have obtained and used the missiles without the open sources of supply and training grounds in Pakistan. Much more importantly, the Stingers proved crucial in reopening the lines from those safe supply dumps and training camps to the fighters in Afghanistan. The missiles helped the Mujahideen in many ways, but they helped on the borders most of all. After 1986 the communists never again came close to cutting the pipelines between Pakistan and Afghanistan.

Soviet Withdrawal, Afghanistan's Half Victory

By the fall of 1986 the Soviets had pretty much decided to give up on their direct role in Afghanistan. Soviet leader Mikhail Gorbachev had initially escalated the war in 1985, but the difficulty of the fighting and the internal structural weaknesses of the Soviet economy had turned the war into a disaster for the Russians. They decided that fall to begin preparations to withdraw troops in the next few years, and they began serious efforts to negotiate a settlement to end the war.

As the Soviets offered peace, they picked up the bombing along the Pakistan border to try to get more favorable conditions. In 1987 such bombings killed and wounded over 1,000 Afghan refugees and Pakistani tribesmen, and even led to some combat between Pakistani and communist aircraft.[91] It was all part of the Soviets last hurrah. On 14 April 1988, the Soviets signed accords at Geneva to set the terms of their withdrawal. They began pulling out troops shortly thereafter, and the last Soviet troops left in February 1989. The Soviet Union continued aid to the communist Afghan government until 1991; the United States continued to aid various rebel groups. When the Soviet Union collapsed and the aid ceased, the communist regime fell. Afghanistan continued to fight its civil war, the United States lost interest, and the fundamentalist Taliban emerged from the fighting to take control of the country until the American invasion in 2001.[92] There were no real winners in the Soviet-Afghan War.

But the Mujahideen did drive out the Soviets, or, perhaps more accurately, the Soviets failed to defeat the Mujahideen insurgency. Plenty of analysts have looked at the war to try to explain the Soviet failure and they have come up with several answers. The Soviets built their army to fight a conventional war in northern Europe and did not have the equipment, structure, or training to fight a counterinsurgency in central Asia. Soviet counterinsurgency doctrine was nonexistent at the beginning of the war, and the scorched earth policies they embraced to pacify the villages did not solve the problem. They did not have a workable plan to create and maintain an effective and independent communist Afghan government and military. And most important of all, the Soviets never invested the resources or manpower necessary to crush the insurgency in a country the size of Afghanistan. For their part, the Mujahideen were tough, dedicated, flexible, and led by many individuals who had a firm grasp of the essentials of guerrilla warfare.[93]

These points all have merit, but together they can leave the misleading impression that the Soviets never really had a chance in the war. In truth, Soviet tactical adjustments to a more fluid style of warfare gave them greater security and made them very effective in direct engagements with the rebels. The destruction of Afghan villages, while morally reprehensible, did create problems for the guerrillas fighting deep in the country. The communist Afghan government and army, while far from efficient, did improve, and maintained general control of the country for years after the Soviets left. And it is unclear whether or not more troops would have made the difference for the Soviets, especially if those troops had been used primarily to defeat the insurgents within Afghanistan. But whatever successes the communists enjoyed in Afghanistan, they never adequately dealt with the problem of the open border with Pakistan.

Some Soviets recognized the importance of this failure. For example two former Soviet officials made perfectly clear how important the open border and sanctuary was to the Mujahideen war:

> Despite the overall heavy losses suffered by the Mujahidin from combat actions by Soviet troops, their organization and strength in Afghanistan did not change particularly, remaining quite stable. This was achieved by constant replenishment of the units due to the arrival of trained troops from Pakistan added to recruiting and conscription in Afghanistan. We estimate that every month, up to eighty groups numbering about 2,000 men were sent into Afghanistan.... Air-defense systems were concentrated in regions along the Pakistan border, where large numbers of rebel troops, bases, camps, and other installations were located. In addition to the Stingers, the air-defense system used cannon of 14.5mm and heavy-caliber 12.7mm machine guns.[94]

Even more striking was the Politburo meeting in November 1986, where Soviet leader Mikhail Gorbachev complained that "We have been fighting in Afghanistan for already six years. If the approach is not changed, we will continue to fight for another 20-30 years." One of his comrades replied, "Too long ago we spoke on the fact that it is necessary to close off the border of Afghanistan with Pakistan and Iran. Experience has shown that we were unable to do this...."[95] The Soviets had come to recognize that if they could not close the border—or would not expend the resources necessary even to try—the war boiled down to who was willing to fight it out the longest. With this recognition came the decision to withdraw.

The toughness, dedication, flexibility, and effectiveness of the Mujahideen guerrilla war is not in doubt, but even the toughest and most dedicated warriors need food, weapons, ammunition, reinforcements, and rest. The Mujahideen always had a ready source of manpower and material, and they always had a safe place to rest and refit. They may have won the war without the sanctuaries and supply lines in Pakistan, but it would have been infinitely more difficult. As one expert on guerilla warfare has argued, "In analyzing this war, it would be impossible to overestimate the importance either of the willingness of foreign powers to supply the insurgents with modern weapons, or the failure of the Soviets to isolate the country from that assistance."[96] Another student of the war put it even more succinctly, "the availability of sanctuaries to the resistance was not merely helpful, it was indispensable."[97]

Endnotes

1. Jimmy Carter, *Keeping Faith: Memoirs of a President* (Toronto: Bantam Books, 1982), 470-471. See also Zbigniew Brzezinski, *Power and Principle: Memoirs of the National Security Advisor, 1977-1981* (New York: Farrar Straus Giroux, 1983), 426.

2. Daily Diary of President Jimmy Carter, 28 December 1979, Jimmy Carter Presidential Library, Online at http://www.jimmycarterlibrary.gov, accessed 30 March 2006.

3. Thomas T. Hammond, *Red Flag Over Afghanistan: The Communist Coup, the Soviet Invasion, and the Consequences* (Boulder, CO: Westview Press, 1984), 105-120.

4. Carter, *Keeping Faith*, 471. On the controversy over the American intelligence community predicting the invasion, see Douglas J. MacEachin, *Predicting the Soviet Invasion of Afghanistan: The Intelligence Community's Record* (Washington, DC: Center for the Study of Intelligence, 2002); Robert M. Gates, *From the Shadows: The Ultimate Insider's Story of Five Presidents and How They Won the Cold War* (New York: Simon and Schuster, 1996), 131-134.

5. A solid geographical description of the country can be found in Scott R. McMichael, *Stumbling Bear: Soviet Military Performance in Afghanistan* (London: Brassey's, 1991), 18-24.

6. A popular summary of Afghanistan's military history is Stephen Tanner, *Afghanistan: A Military History from Alexander the Great to the Fall of the Taliban* (New York: Da Capo Press, 2002).

7. More detailed descriptions of the lead-up, motivations, and actions of the Soviet invasion can be found in M. Hassan Kakar, *Afghanistan: The Soviet Invasion and the Afghan Response, 1979-1982* (Berkeley: University of California Press, 1995), 1-50; Odd Arne Westad, *"Concerning the Situation is 'A': New Russian Evidence on the Soviet Intervention in Afghanistan,"* and "The Soviet Union and Afghanistan, 1978-1989," *Cold War International History Project Bulletin*, 8/9 (Winter 1996), 128-161; Amin Saikal, *Modern Afghanistan: A History of Struggle and Survival* (London: I.B. Tauris, 2004), 1-197; Mark Galeotti, *Afghanistan: The Soviet Union's Last War* (London: Frank Cass, 1995), 1-20; Vasiliy Mitrokin, *The KGB in Afghanistan*, Working Paper No. 40, (Washington, DC: Cold War International History Project, 2002), 17-113; Anthony Arnold, *The Fateful Pebble: Afghanistan's Role in the Fall of the Soviet Empire* (Novato, CA: Presidio Press, 1993), 1-104; Oleg Sarin and Lev Dvoretsky, *The Afghan Syndrome: The Soviet Union's Vietnam* (Novato, CA: Presidio Press, 1993), 1-41; Christopher Andrew and Vasili Mitrokin, *The World Was Going Our Way: The KGB and the Battle for the Third World* (New York: Basic Books, 2005), 386-402; Christopher Andrew and Oleg Gordievsky, *KGB: The Inside Story*

(New York: HarperCollins, 1990), 573-576; Edward Girardet, *Afghanistan: The Soviet War* (New York: St. Martin's Press, 1985), 12-29; J. Bruce Amstutz, *Afghanistan: The First Five Years of Soviet Occupation* (Washington, DC: National Defense University Press, 1986), 1-49; Mark Urban, *War in Afghanistan* (New York: St. Martin's Press, 1988), 1-50; Hammond, *Red Flag*, 3-102; Raimo Vayrynen, "Afghanistan," *Journal of Peace Research*, 17 (1980), 93-102; Jiri Valenta, "From Prague to Kabul: The Soviet Style of Invasion," *International Security*, 5 (Autumn 1980), 114-141; David Gibbs, "Does the USSR Have a 'Grand Strategy'? Reinterpreting the Invasion of Afghanistan," *Journal of Peace Research*, 24 (December 1987), 365-379; Alam Payind, "Soviet-Afghan Relations from Cooperation to Occupation," *International Journal of Middle East Studies*, 21 (February 1989), 107-128; United States Central Command, *A Brief History of Russian and Soviet Expansion Toward the South*, June 1985, Microfiche 01632, National Security Archive, *Afghanistan: The Making of U.S. Policy, 1973-1990*, (Alexandria, VA: Chadwyck-Healey, 1990); MacEachin, *Predicting*, 1-44; Keith D. Dickson, "The Basmachi and the Mujahidin: Soviet Responses to Insurgency Movements," *Military Review*, 65 (February 1985), 29-44; Anthony James Joes, *America and Guerilla Warfare* (Lexington: University Press of Kentucky, 2000), 279-285.

8. On the early stages of direct Soviet control and for biographical sketches of many of the major players, see Amstutz, *Afghanistan*, 51-86.

9. On the deplorable conditions in Afghanistan and the resulting refugee crisis see Jeri Laber and Barnett R. Rubin, *"A Nation is Dying": Afghanistan Under the Soviets, 1979-87* (Evanston, IL: Northwestern University Press, 1988); Olivier Roy, *Islam and Resistance in Afghanistan*, 2d edition (Cambridge University Press, 1990), 165-171; Girardet, *Afghanistan*, 202-232; Nancy Hatch Dupree, "Demographic Reporting on Afghan Refugees in Pakistan," *Modern Asian Studies*, 22 (1988), 845-865; Kurt Lohbeck, *Holy War, Unholy Victory: Eyewitness to the CIA's Secret War in Afghanistan* (Washington, DC: Regnery, 1993), passim; Grant M. Farr and John G. Merriam, eds., *Afghan Resistance: The Politics of Survival* (Boulder, CO: Westview Press, 1987), 127-212; Amstutz, *Afghanistan*, 223-321; Kakar, *Afghanistan*, passim; Urban, *War in Afghanistan*, 157-158; Joes, *America and Guerilla Warfare*, 305-306.

10. The term Mujahideen is Arabic for "struggler." Looser translations include "holy warrior" or "freedom fighter." The word is transliterated many ways.

11. "The Afghan Resistance: Struggling for Unity," CIA Assessment, June 1984, CIA FOIA, Online: http://www.foia.cia.gov, (accessed 29 March 2006); Shah M. Tarzi, "Politics of the Afghan Resistance Movement," *Asian Survey*, 31 (June 1991), 479-495; Tahir Amin, "Afghan Resistance: Past, Present, and Future," *Asian Survey*, 24 (April 1984), 373-399; Amstutz, *Afghanistan*, 92-101.

12. Urban, *War in Afghanistan*, 95-97.

13. Zalmay Khalilzad, "Soviet-Occupied Afghanistan," *Problems of Communism*, 29 (Nov-Dec 1980), 35-39; Steve Coll, *Ghost Wars: The Secret History of the CIA, Afghanistan, and Bin Laden, from the Soviet Invasion to September 10, 2001* (New York: Penguin Books, 2004),107-124; Amstutz, *Afghanistan*, 112-115; and Joes, *America and Guerilla Warfare*, 285-289.

14. An early attempt to unify the resistance parties under the leadership of Sayyaf quickly fell apart. Urban, *War in Afghanistan*, 59, 77, 82-83. See also Roy, *Islam and Resistance in Afghanistan*, passim; Olivier Roy, *Afghanistan: From Holy War to Civil War* (Princeton, NJ: Darwin Press, 1995), 11-59; Coll, *Ghost Wars*, 71-88; and Alexandre Bennigsen, "Mullahs, Mujahidin and Soviet Muslims," *Problems of Communism*, 33 (November-December 1984), 28-44.

15. On international law aspects of the invasion see W. Michael Reisman and James Silk, "Which Law Applies to the Afghan Conflict?" *American Journal of International Law*, 82 (July 1988), 459-486. See also Amstutz, *Afghanistan*, 199-222.

16. The Saudis often worked independent of the United States and even Pakistan in order to aid the radical Muslim groups more directly. It was through this independent pipeline that Osama bin Laden became involved in the war. Coll, *Ghost Wars*, 71-88.

17. John G. Merriam, "Arms Shipments to the Afghan Resistance," in Farr and Merriam, eds., *Afghan Resistance*, 71-101; Hammond, *Red Flag*, 157-158; Amstutz, *Afghanistan*, 206-207.

18. Coll, *Ghost Wars*, 42-50; Gates, *From the Shadows*, 143-147; Joe Stork, "U.S. Involvement in Afghanistan," *MERIP Reports*, 89 (July-August 1980), 25-26.

19. The invasion also led to the United States canceling the SALT II talks, imposing economic sanctions on the Soviet Union, and boycotting the 1980 Summer Olympics in Moscow. Jimmy Carter, "State of the Union Address," 23 January 1980, *Public Papers of the Presidents*, The American Presidency Project, Online: http://www.presidency.ucsb.edu, (accessed 5 May 2006). For more on Carter, his administration, and their response to the invasion, including critiques, see Carter, *Keeping Faith*, 470-489; Brzezinski, *Power and Principle*, 428-437; Christopher Andrew, *For the President's Eyes Only: Secret Intelligence and the American Presidency from Washington to Bush* (New York: HarperCollins, 1995), 447-448; Burton I. Kaufman, *The Presidency of James Earl Carter, Jr.* (Lawrence: University Press of Kansas, 1993), 162-166; Gaddis Smith, *Morality, Reason, and Power: American Diplomacy in the Carter Years* (New York: Hill and Wang, 1986), 222-231; William Stueck, "Placing Jimmy Carter's Foreign Policy," in *The Carter Presidency: Policy Choices in the Post-New Deal Era*, edited by Gary M. Fink and Hugh Davis Graham, (Lawrence: University Press of Kansas, 1999), 256-259; David Skidmore, "Carter and the Failure of

Foreign Policy Reform," *Political Science Quarterly*, 108 (Winter 1993-1994), 722-729; Hammond, *Red Flag*, 120-122. Secretary of State Cyrus Vance was the most important member of the administration who demurred from Carter's response to the invasion. Cyrus Vance, *Hard Choices: Critical Years in America's Foreign Policy* (New York: Simon and Schuster, 1983), 384-397.

20. Quoted in Coll, *Ghost Wars*, 51.

21. Quoted in Urban, *War in Afghanistan*, 57.

22. Coll, *Ghost Wars*, 57-58. See also Gates, *From the Shadows*, 147-149; and Alexander Alexiev, *The United States and the War in Afghanistan* (Santa Monica, CA: RAND, 1988).

23. Quoted in Coll, *Ghost Wars*, 51 (emphasis added).

24. "Iranian Support to the Afghan Resistance," Defense Intelligence Agency Paper, 11 July 1985, National Security Archive, George Washington University, Online: http://www.gwu.edu/~nsarchiv; "Iran-Afghanistan: Military Tensions," CIA Report, 21 November 1983, CIA FOIA, Online: http://www.foia.cia.gov, (accessed 29 March 2006); Roy, *Afghanistan*, 100; Alvin Z. Rubinstein, "The Soviet Union and Iran Under Khomeini," *International Affairs*, 57 (Autumn 1981), 599-617; Rasul Bakhsh Rais, "Afghanistan and the Regional Powers," *Asian Survey*, 33 (September 1993), 916-919.

25. Urban, *War in Afghanistan*, 97.

26. Christopher S. Wren, "Soviet is Assailed on Afghan Policy," *New York Times*, 28 December 1982, A7; "Peking Hails Cause of Rebels in Cambodia and Afghanistan," *New York Times*, 14 December 1982, A3; Urban, *War in Afghanistan*, 123; Yaacov Vertzberger, "Afghanistan in China's Policy," *Problems of Communism*, 31 (May-June 1982), 1-23; "The Wakhan Corridor: An Unlikely Afghan-China Link," CIA Research Paper, May 1980, National Security Archive, Microfiche 0933; Leslie Holmes, "Afghanistan and Sino-Soviet Relations," in *The Soviet Withdrawal from Afghanistan*, edited by Amin Saikal and William Maley, (Cambridge University Press, 1989), 122-141.

27. Reisman and Silk, "Which Law," 478.

28. Quoted in Coll, *Ghost Wars*, 51. From the beginning of the war many in the American intelligence community was acutely concerned with keeping the border open, although some initial assessments thought the rebels controlled enough territory within Afghanistan to not need Pakistan. See "The Afghan Insurgents and Pakistan: Problems for Islamabad and Moscow," CIA Intelligence Memorandum, 1 January 1980, CIA FOIA, Online: http://www.foia.cia.gov, (accessed 17 May 2006); "Prospects for Closing the Afghan-Pakistan Border," CIA Intelligence Assessment, July 1981, National Security Archive, Microfiche 01214. By April 1983, the CIA had produced an extensive guide to the passes all along the border, "Passes and Trails on the Pakistan-Afghanistan Border," CIA Reference Aid, April 1983, National Security Archive, Microfiche 01447.

29. On the difficult diplomatic situation for Pakistan and the other supporters of the Mujahideen, see W. Howard Wriggins, "Pakistan's Search for a Foreign Policy After the Invasion of Afghanistan," *Pacific Affairs*, 57 (Summer 1984), 284-303; Ahmed Rashid, "Pakistan, Afghanistan and the Gulf," *MERIP Middle East Report*, (September-October 1987), 35-39; Edgar O'Ballance, "Pakistan: On the Front Porch of Conflict," *Military Review*, 66 (March 1986), 68-75; Marvin G. Weinbaum, "Pakistan and Afghanistan: The Strategic Relationship," *Asian Survey*, 31 (June 1991), 496-511; Stephen P. Cohen, "South Asia After Afghanistan," *Problems of Communism*, 34 (January-February 1985), 18-31; Rais, "Afghanistan and the Regional Powers," 906-912.

30. Barnett R. Rubin, *The Search for Peace in Afghanistan: From Buffer State to Failed State* (New Haven, CT: Yale University Press, 1995), 38.

31. To facilitate a better working relationship with Pakistan, the US also gave considerable military aid to the Pakistanis and basically ignored the developing Pakistani nuclear program. See Coll, *Ghost Wars*, 58-64; Mohammad Yousaf and Mark Adkin, *Afghanistan—The Bear Trap: The Defeat of a Superpower* (Havertown, PA: Casemate, 2001), passim; Theodore L. Eliot and Robert L. Pfaltzgraff, eds., *The Red Army on Pakistan's Border: Policy Implications for the United States* (Washington, DC: Pergamon-Brassey's, 1986); Jeffrey Richelson, *The U.S. Intelligence Community*, 2d edition, (Cambridge, MA: Ballinger Publishing, 1989), 342-343; Charles G. Cogan, "Partners in Time: The CIA and Afghanistan since 1979," *World Policy Journal*, 10 (Summer 1993), 73-82; Jamal Rashid, "Pakistan and the Central Command," *MERIP Middle East Report*, 141 (July-August 1986), 28-34; T.V. Paul, "Influence Through Arms Transfers: Lessons from the U.S.-Pakistani Relationship," *Asian Survey*, 32 (December 1992), 1078-1092.

32. Yousaf and Adkin, *Afghanistan*, 49.

33. Girardet, *Afghanistan*, 63-64.

34. Ibid., 64.

35. McMichael, *Stumbling Bear*, 27-31.

36. Roy, *Islam and Resistance*, 183.

37. Ali Ahmad Jalali and Lester W. Grau, eds., *Afghan Guerilla Warfare: In the Words of the Mujahideen Fighters* (London: Compendium, 2001); passim; Girardet, *Afghanistan*, 48-68; McMichael, *Stumbling Bear*, 32-37; Amstutz, *Afghanistan*, 134-138.

38. Khalilzad, "Soviet-Occupied Afghanistan," 31.

39. For more detailed and nuanced discussions of Soviet tactics see Lester W. Grau, ed., *The Bear Went Over the Mountain: Soviet Combat Tactics in Afghanistan* (Washington, DC: National Defense University Press, 1996); Robert F. Baumann, *Russian-Soviet Unconventional Wars in the Caucasus, Central Asia, and Afghanistan*, Leavenworth Paper Number 20, (Fort Leavenworth, KS: Com-

bat Studies Institute, 1993), 138-143; Zalmay Khalilzad, "Moscow's Afghan War," *Problems of Communism*, 35 (January-February 1986), 1-10; Lester W. Grau and Mohammand Yahya Nawroz, "The Soviet Experience in Afghanistan," *Military Review*, 75 (September-October 1995), 16-27; Edgar O'Ballance, "Soviet Tactics in Afghanistan," *Military Review*, 60 (August 1980), 45-52; Sarin and Dvoretsky, *Afghan Syndrome*, 87-121; Kip McCormick, "The Evolution of Soviet Military Doctrine, Afghanistan," *Military Review*, 67 (July 1987), 61-72; McMichael, *Stumbling Bear*, 38-79; Galeotti, *Afghanistan*, 190-206; Girardet, *Afghanistan*, 30-36; Urban, *War in Afghanistan*, 66-68, 119-120; Amstutz, *Afghanistan*, 148-152.

40. Quoted in Coll, *Ghost Wars*, 122.

41. Roy, *Islam and Resistance*, 139-148.

42. Urban, *War in Afghanistan*, 100.

43. Hammond, *Red Flag*, 161-162.

44. On these atrocities, and much more, see Laber and Rubin, *A Nation is Dying*, passim, (the quotation is on page 42); Andrew and Gordievsky, *KGB*, 576-578.

45. Amstutz, *Afghanistan*, 192-193.

46. Urban, *War in Afghanistan*, 101-109, 118-119, 143-148.

47. For more detail on Soviet counterinsurgency doctrine, including attempts to infiltrate and subvert the rebel movements, see Amstutz, *Afghanistan*, 144-148.

48. Jalali and Grau, eds., *Afghan Guerrilla*, 402-403.

49. "Report by Soviet Minister Ustinov to CPSU CC on 'Foreign Interference' in Afghanistan," 2 October 1980, and "A Report by Soviet Military Intelligence," 1 September 1981, Cold War International History Project, Online: http:/www.wilsoncenter.org, (accessed 28 March 2006).

50. "Pakistan Says Raid By Afghans Killed 40," *New York Times*, 29 January 1984, A5; "Pakistan Says Afghans Have Killed 104 in Raids," *New York Times*, 23 August 1984, A5; Girardet, *Afghanistan*, 36-37; Urban, *War in Afghanistan*, 90-91.

51. Urban, *War in Afghanistan*, 91.

52. Richard M. Weintraub, "Pakistan's Frontier Is Drawn Into War," *Washington Post*, 25 March 1987, A15. See also Vladimir Kuzichkin, *Inside the KGB: My Life in Soviet Espionage* (New York: Pantheon Books, 1990), 349-350; Mitrokin, *KGB in Afghanistan*, 138-148; Andrew and Mitrokin, *The World Was Going Our Way*, 355-367; and McMichael, *Stumbling Bear*, 107-108.

53. Quoted in Amstutz, *Afghanistan*, 144.

54. Kuzichkin, *Inside the KGB*, 349.

55. Ibid., 349.

56. McMichael, *Stumbling Bear*, 103-107.

57. Urban, *War in Afghanistan*, 91-93, 156-157, 186-188.

58. Frederick Kempe, "Soviet 'Hot Pursuit' of Guerrillas into Pakistan Could Draw Islamabad into Afghan Fighting," *Wall Street Journal*, 12 November 1984, 1.

59. Yousaf and Adkin, *Afghanistan*, 162-164; Urban, *War in Afghanistan*, 176-179.

60. Lee O. Coldren, "Afghanistan in 1985: The Sixth Year of the Russo-Afghan War," *Asian Survey*, 26 (February 1986), 242.

61. Jalali and Grau, eds., *Afghan Guerrilla*, 317-326; Yousaf and Adkin, *Afghanistan*, 166-173; Baumann, *Russian-Soviet Unconventional Wars*, 145-147; Urban, *War in Afghanistan*, 190-194.

62. Coll, *Ghost Wars*, 69. An excellent description of the growing difficulty of the trip into Afghanistan is Frederick Kempe, "Risky Mission: Supplying Guerrillas in Afghanistan is Grueling Undertaking," *Wall Street Journal*, 14 November 1984, 1.

63. Rashid, "Pakistan, Afghanistan," 37.

64. Milt Beardon and James Rosen, *The Main Enemy: The Inside Story of the CIA's Final Showdown with the KGB* (New York: Random House, 2003), 207; Coll, *Ghost Wars*, 133-134.

65. Quoted in Girardet, *Afghanistan*, 65.

66. Rosanne Klass, "Pushing and Pulling Apart Pakistan," *Wall Street Journal*, 2 October 1984, 1.

67. Ronald Reagan, "Radio Address to the Nation on the Soviet Occupation of Afghanistan," 28 December 1985, Ronald Reagan Presidential Library, Online: http://www.reagan.utexas.edu, (accessed 4 April 2006); W. Eliot Brownlee and Hugh Davis Graham, eds., *The Reagan Presidency: Pragmatic Conservatism and Its Legacies* (Lawrence: University Press of Kansas, 2003), 85-152; Doyle McManus, "U.S. Shaping Assertive Policy for Third World," *Los Angeles Times*, 16 June 1985, 1; Lou Cannon, *President Reagan: The Role of a Lifetime* (New York: Simon and Schuster, 1991); Peter Schweizer, *Reagan's War: The Epic Story of His Forty-Year Struggle and Final Triumph Over Communism* (New York: Doubleday, 2002); George P. Shultz, *Turmoil and Triumph: My Years as Secretary of State* (New York: Charles Scribner's Sons, 1993); and William J. Daugherty, *Executive Secrets: Covert Action and the Presidency* (Lexington: University Press of Kentucky, 2004), 193-211.

68. Rubin, *Search for Peace*, 30; Gates, *From the Shadows*, 251-252.

69. Richelson, *U.S. Intelligence Community*, 341.

70. George Crile, *Charlie Wilson's War* (New York: Grove Press, 2003), passim.

71. Steve Coll, "Anatomy of a Victory: CIA's Covert Afghan War," *Washington Post*, 19 July 1992, A1; Gates, *From the Shadows*, 319-321.

72. Rubin, *Search for Peace*, 30; Richelson, *U.S. Intelligence*, 340-343.

73. Coll, *Ghost Wars*, 125-132; Robert Pear, "Arming Afghan Guerrillas: A Huge Effort Led by U.S.," *New York Times*, 18 April 1988, A1; Gates, *From the Shadows*, 348-349; Beardon and Rosen, *Main Enemy*, 210.

74. Jalali and Grau, eds., *Afghan Guerilla*, 403-404; "CIA Reportedly Flies Texas Mules to Afghan Rebels," *Los Angeles Times*, 19 October 1987, 8.

75. Gates, *From the Shadows*, 349.

76. More details on the importation and standards of mules in the war see Beardon and Rosen, *Main Enemy*, 310-314.

77. "The Soviet Invasion of Afghanistan: Five Years After," CIA Assessment, 1 May 1985, CIA FOIA, Online: http://www.foia.cia.gov, (accessed 29 March 2006), 18.

78. McMichael, *Stumbling Bear*, 89-90.

79. Urban, *War in Afghanistan*, 162-163.

80. Beardon and Rosen, *Main Enemy*, 245; McMichael, *Stumbling Bear*, 90.

81. The debate over the whether or not to distribute the Stinger is ably covered in Alan J. Kuperman, "The Stinger Missile and U.S. Intervention in Afghanistan," *Political Science Quarterly*, 114 (Summer 1999), 219-263; and John Walcott and Tim Carrington, "Role Reversal: CIA Resisted Proposal to Give Afghan Rebels U.S. Stinger Missiles," *Wall Street Journal*, 16 February 1988, 1.

82. Coll, *Ghost Wars*, 11; Gates, *From the Shadows*, 349-350. CIA agent Milt Beardon oversaw much of the distribution of the Stingers in the war. His story is recounted in Beardon and Rosen, *Main Enemy*, 212-367.

83. John H. Cushman, "The Stinger Missile: Helping to Change the Course of a War," *New York Times*, 17 January 1988, A2.

84. Richelson, *U.S. Intelligence*, 341.

85. Baumann, *Russian-Soviet Unconventional War*, 155.

86. Beardon and Rosen, *Main Enemy*, 246-254; Schweizer, *Reagan's War*, 256-257.

87. Figures on the numbers of communist planes shot down vary and some observers have downplayed the effectiveness of the Stingers, noting that the Soviets created effective countermeasures and were already in the process of drawing down their forces when the Stingers came online. See Urban, *War in Afghanistan*, 296; Galeotti, *Afghanistan*, 195-196; and Gilles Dorronsoro, *Revolution Unending: Afghanistan: 1979 to the Present* (New York: Columbia University Press, 2005), 208. No doubt the Stinger did not win the war on its own, but the evidence is overwhelming that the Soviets had stepped up their efforts along the border in 1984-1986; that the Stinger did cause severe damage to communist airpower; and that it therefore did play an essential role in reopening infiltration routes. The best discussion of all issue relating to the Stinger in Afghanistan is Kuperman, "The Stinger Missile," 244-263. See also U.S. Army Report, "Impact of the Stinger Missile on Soviet and Resistance Tactics in AF," March 1987,

National Security Archive, Microfiche 01936; United States Central Command, "Stinger: One Year of Combat," 26 October 1987, National Security Archive, Microfiche 02065; Aaron Karp, "Blowpipes and Stingers in Afghanistan: One Year Later," *Armed Forces Journal International*, 125 (September 1987), 36-40; Michael Mecham, "U.S. Credits Afghan Resistance with Thwarting Soviet Airpower," *Aviation Week and Space Technology*, 127 (13 July 1987), 26-27; William J. Eaton, "Stingers Take Heavy Toll in Afghanistan," *Los Angeles Times*, 21 January 1987, 5; David B. Ottaway, "U.S. Missiles Alter War in Afghanistan," *Washington Post*, 19 July 1987, A1; Yousaf and Adkin, *Afghanistan*, 174-188; McMichael, *Stumbling Bear*, 90-91; Arnold, *Fateful Pebble*, 138-139.

88. Roy, *Islam and Resistance*, 209.

89. Gates, *From the Shadows*, 430.

90. Beardon and Rosen, *Main Enemy*, 254. Charles Dunbar also noticed the morale boost that came from the introduction of Stingers, "Afghanistan in 1986: The Balance Endures," *Asian Survey*, 27 (February 1987), 129.

91. Rashid, "Pakistan, Afghanistan," 35-36; Elaine Sciolino, "Afghan Air Raids Against Pakistan are Said to Kill 85," *New York Times*, 25 March 1987, A8; Barbara Crossette, "Pakistan Downs an Afghan Intruder," *New York Times*, 31 March 1987, A3; Weintraub, "Pakistan's Frontier," *Washington Post*, A15.

92. Coll, *Ghost Wars*, 158-584; Rubin, *Search for Peace*, passim; Saikal and Maley, eds., *Soviet Withdrawal*, passim; Diego Cordovez and Selig S. Harrison, *Out of Afghanistan: The Inside Story of the Soviet Withdrawal* (New York: Oxford University Press, 1995), passim; Riaz M. Khan, *Untying the Afghan Knot: Negotiating Soviet Withdrawal* (Durham, NC: Duke University Press, 1991), passim; Don Oberdorfer, *The Turn: From the Cold War to a New Era* (New York: Poseidon Press, 1991), 234-243, 269-282; Sarah E. Mendelson, "Internal Battles and External Wars: Politics, Learning, and the Soviet Withdrawal from Afghanistan," *World Politics*, 45 (April 1993), 327-360; Ted Daley, "Afghanistan and Gorbachev's Global Foreign Policy," *Asian Survey*, 29 (May 1989), 496-513; Richard K. Herrmann, "Soviet Behavior in Regional Conflicts: Old Questions, New Strategies, and Important Lessons," *World Politics*, 44 (April 1992), 432-465; Theodore L. Eliot, "Afghanistan in 1989: Stalemate," *Asian Survey*, 30 (February 1990), 158-166;

93. These general conclusions comprise a summary of the common arguments found in the sources cited throughout this chapter.

94. Sarin and Dvoretsky, *Afghan Syndrome*, 101.

95. "Communist Party Soviet Union Central Committee Politburo transcript," 13 November 1986, "The Soviet Union and Afghanistan, 1978-1989," *Cold War International History Project Bulletin*, 8/9 (Winter 1996), 178-179.

96. Joes, *America and Guerrilla Warfare*, 313.

97. Robert F. Baumann, "Compound Warfare Case Study: The Soviets in Afghanistan," in Huber, ed., *Compound Warfare*, 295.

Conclusion

Vietnam and Afghanistan Compared

Vietnam and Afghanistan were profoundly different, yet transnational sanctuaries were vital to the insurgencies in both wars. In Vietnam, the communists were a well-developed and multifaceted enemy. In the words of two prominent Vietnam historians, "The enemy was no rag-tag band lurking in the jungle, but rather a combination of guerrillas, political cadre, and modern main-force units...."[1] The insurgency was a large part of the fight, especially early on, but it needed the efforts of the conventional forces in order to survive. The insurgency faltered after 1968, when the Americans and South Vietnamese took advantage of a weakened Vietcong to engage in serious efforts to pacify and provide security for the countryside. Then the communist conventional forces picked up their efforts. And, ultimately, it was a conventional invasion that overran the South and won the war for the communists.

The same was most assuredly not the case in the Soviet war in Afghanistan. The Mujahideen fought a strictly insurgent war. There was no unified political cadre among the resistances, and they certainly never brought any kind of conventional force into the field. For their part, the communists never controlled the countryside and never engaged in any kind of real effort to win the hearts and minds of the people of Afghanistan. But they did seek to tilt the demographic situation in the country in their favor. The Soviets hunted down and killed thousands of guerillas and they pursued a scorched earth policy toward supposedly unfriendly villages within Afghanistan. Their policies drove millions of potentially hostile Afghans out of the country and made it much harder for the Mujahideen to thrive as a fighting force in the hinterlands. However, they did thrive in the borderlands, and they did thrive when they had some sort of connection with the outside world.

In Vietnam and Afghanistan, the United States and the Soviet Union used drastically different tactics to fight their respective insurgencies. It must be stated that the United States enjoyed much more success on that score. Even though the Soviets succeeded in pacifying areas of the countryside, their methods ensured that the countryside remained unfriendly. The people in rural areas of Vietnam may not have grown to love the United States and the South Vietnamese government, but they became much less unfriendly in the later years of the war as the allies began to provide for their safety from the Vietcong. In a comparison of counterinsurgency techniques, the American effort proved superior to Soviet methods.

However, had those NVA conventional forces not made use of the sanctuaries in Laos and Cambodia to invade the South, it is still unclear whether the American counterinsurgency would have succeeded in Vietnam. Those sanctuaries ensured that, at the very least, the communist guerrillas would have been able to wage low-level assaults within South Vietnam for as long as they wanted. As long as they had the sanctuaries and the ability to cross over the border, the war would have been an even more prolonged battle of wills. It did not happen that way because the communists had the resources and organization to use the sanctuaries to launch conventional attacks, but in either case, clear victory could only have been obtained by denying the communists those sanctuaries.

The same went for the Soviets in Afghanistan. Even though their brutal treatment of the population was less effective than American pacification techniques in Vietnam, it did have some effect. To whatever the degree their scorched earth tactics denied the Mujahideen sanctuary within Afghanistan, those tactics did not address the problem of sanctuary in Pakistan. And so the Mujahideen could rest, refit, plan, and launch new attacks across the border indefinitely, especially once the Stinger missiles helped clear the skies above the frontier. The battle of wills for Afghanistan depended on sanctuary; the Mujahideen kept the sanctuary and won that battle.[2]

None of this is to say that the techniques for fighting the counterinsurgency in-country do not matter. The Americans were much closer to success in Vietnam than the Soviets ever were in Afghanistan. Indeed, denying the insurgents sanctuary at home is a necessary first condition for a successful counterinsurgency. However, it is not the last condition. As long as the guerrillas have a safe place to which to retreat and rest, and from which to gather resources and launch new attacks, they can fight as long as they have the will to keep on fighting.[3]

Sanctuary Doctrine

Sanctuary did not become less of an issue in irregular warfare in the last decades of the 20th century. In the late 1970s and early 1980s, guerrillas in Israel hid behind the Lebanese border. At the same time, Marxist rebels in El Salvador relied on outside support from Cuba and the Soviet Union.

Nicaraguan Contras operated with American aid out of Honduras in the 1980s. In Africa, rebels frequently found refuge and support in neighboring states in the upheavals throughout the continent in those years. Even the end of the Cold War did not bring an end to active sanctuary. Dozens of wars in the 1990s, large and small, saw outside powers give support to insurgent efforts, many of them through transnational sanctuaries.[4]

All of these conflicts have meant that there is no shortage of literature on the topic. Historically the American military preferred to focus on large conventional operations, but in the years since the onset of the Vietnam War Americans have invested serious time and effort in learning the lessons of small wars and counterinsurgencies. Experts in and out of uniform have written on the issue of transnational sanctuary in insurgent warfare. As early as 1962, historians Peter Paret and John Shy wrote that guerrillas needed bases of operation, and that for insurgents, "there is little evidence that victory can be gained without [foreign assistance]."[5] Bernard Fall's body of work on the French in Indochina stressed the importance of sanctuary, and in 1967, J. J. Zasloff looked at Chinese aid to the Vietminh and concluded that it might not have been the essential feature of the communist victory, but it certainly helped.[6] Marine MAJ G. R. Christmas wrote a 1973 article in *Infantry* magazine on the issue and concluded, "One fact remains incontrovertible. It is vital to any nation's survival that the guerrilla be denied sanctuary and external support in the form of arms and equipment if he is to be destroyed."[7]

Many of these early works were vague or contained few suggestions of how to deal with the problem, but that began to change by the end of the 1970s. Professor John Deiner looked at the problem in 1979 and emphasized "border control and armed incursion."[8] Marine officer John Hamilton wrote a paper for the Marine Corps Command and Staff College in 1985 that outlined the transnational sanctuary issue and strongly recommended that the US military develop high technology border barrier capabilities.[9] In 1995 insurgency expert Steven Metz wrote that a key principle of counterinsurgency was what he called "secondary support." He recommended that the "United States might lead efforts to deter, isolate, and punish external sponsors of insurgency."[10] More specifically, a recent article by political scientist Paul Staniland also advocated "fences, surveillance, and aggressive pursuit along vulnerable sections" of the border, along with a sustained public diplomacy effort to delegitimize "the transnational pillar of the insurgency…"[11]

Yet for all the examples, official American military counterinsurgency doctrine has focused very little attention on solving the problem of transnational sanctuary.[12] The original Army field manual on counterguerrilla operations suggested that indigenous forces should watch borders "to economize on the available (US) military combat power which can be better utilized against the guerrilla force."[13] Even the 1968 manual on denial barriers focused more on barriers as part of conventional operations.[14] The 1986 version of *Counterguerrilla Operations* spent more time on borders, but again emphasized the use of civilian security forces or populations to protect the frontiers. The section on sanctuaries reads, in full:

> Guerrillas may establish base camps and conduct cross-border operations from countries adjacent to the host country. They will take advantage of an international boundary to launch operations or evade pursuit with impunity. Commanders operating in border areas must respect the sanctity of international boundaries, but they can conduct combat operations against the guerrilla force once it crosses back over the border. Ambush patrols are an excellent means of dealing with guerrillas who attempt to use an international border as a sanctuary.[15]

The paragraph indicated the difficulty for military commanders on the ground, but offered little by way of advice.

In the 1990s American strategists came to a greater acceptance of counterinsurgencies and stability operations as an essential part of the responsibilities of the US military. By the turn of the 21st century, writers of doctrine began to weave together conventional and unconventional operations. Even then, they spent little time on the vital importance of denying insurgents transnational sanctuary.16 As a result, American leaders and military commanders in the global war on terrorism have had little doctrinal guidance on the topic.

The Contemporary Picture

Stability operations continue apace in Afghanistan and Iraq. Despite some setbacks in both theaters, the United States military has put its experience and study of counterinsurgency and contingency operations to good use. Moreover, it is clear that at the highest levels of American leadership there has been recognition that the terrorists have been using international borders to find refuge and resupply. As a result, there have been some efforts to close down the borders and deny sanctuary. However, without clear doctrinal understanding of the importance of transnational sanctuaries, these efforts have been haphazard and incomplete.

It is certainly worth noting that the current effort in Afghanistan, while not easy, has been smoother than the ongoing campaigns in Iraq. No doubt, operations in Afghanistan have been aided by the decisiveness of the original campaign to wrest the country from the Taliban, the significant international contribution to peacekeeping efforts, and the ability of homegrown leaders and warlords to control the countryside. However, given the effectiveness and relentlessness of the Mujahideen struggle against the Soviets, it would seem that dedicated guerrillas like the fundamentalist terrorists would have the ability to be more effective themselves. And indeed all reports indicate that they have returned to the old Mujahideen stomping grounds along the Pakistan-Afghanistan border for use as base areas in their war against Afghanistan and the United States. Yet by and large they have not been able to recreate the successes of the anti-Soviet guerrillas, and many of the casualties they have inflicted have been in defensive operations against coalition attacks on their mountain refuges.

What changed? First, the dissipated strands of al-Qaeda and the Taliban do not enjoy the support of any great, or not so great, outside power. No wealthy states are overtly bankrolling their operations or directly providing them with weapons, ammunition, and other supplies. Second, to the extent that minor powers are sympathetic to the terrorist efforts in Afghanistan, those outside powers do not have ready routes by which to supply the insurgent forces. As in the Soviet war, the open terrain of western Afghanistan, and Iran's unstable relationship with the terrorists in Afghanistan have resulted in relative quiet in the western part of the country since the fall of the Taliban.[17]

Just as important, the United States has had the good fortune that the official state apparatus of Pakistan, led by President Pervez Musharraf, has been an ally in the global war on terrorism. While the Pakistanis have not completely closed down and cleared the border with Afghanistan, most of the fighting is in southern Afghanistan, and while there has been some friction over US and Afghan strikes at rebel bases along the frontier, such issues are a far cry from Pakistan's all but open support of the Mujahideen during the Soviet war. The terrorists are dedicated; they have some money; and they have some stockpiles of weapons, but they do not have the full backing of international powers; and they do not have open and safe sanctuaries where they can rest and refit to continue their war.[18]

On the other hand, stability operations in Iraq have been fraught with difficulties. The insurgency there took on a ferocity that surprised many of the war planners, and as a result, the years after the end of the major conventional operations in May 2003 have seen ongoing and often brutal violence.[19] Altogether, untold numbers of Iraqi civilians and security forces, and over 2,000 Americans have died in the fighting for Iraq.

Yet after a fitful start, the American military has done a notable job of learning from the counterinsurgencies of the past and applying those lessons to the fight in Iraq.[20] In a country marked by ethnic and sectarian strife, members of the coalition have made every effort not to alienate the Iraqi civilian population. The dismantling of Saddam Hussein's security apparatus may have slowed the process of allowing the Iraqis to provide for their own security, but it may also have been a necessary step in earning the trust of the Iraqi people. After all, Saddam's troops and police were the tools of Saddam's tyranny. And despite the delays, the coalition effort has begun to show real results. Thousands of guerrillas have been killed or detained. The insurgents have grown frustrated with attempts to target Americans and turned much of their violence first toward Iraqi security forces and more recently toward the civilian population. The insurgency has failed to stop any of the elections in Iraq and it has not caused the country to decline into an all-out civil war.

However, the insurgency does continue to wreak havoc on internal security, which threatens to upset the delicate balance in Iraq. Estimates of the size of the insurgency are at best educated guesses, but the best guesses indicate that despite taking heavy casualties, the overall number of insurgents in Iraq did not significantly decline from 2004 to the spring of 2006.21 No doubt the guerrillas have recruited from the Iraqi population, but it also very likely that they have been replenished from across the borders. At the same time, the weapons used by the insurgents have grown more complex, and some observers insist that the new weaponry and explosives come from Syria and Iran. Coalition efforts on the borders, including the use of diplomatic pressure, sensors, aerial observation, checkpoints, and a variety of other techniques, have not stemmed the tide. This external support for the terrorists does not approach anything like what the communists received in Vietnam, or what the Mujahideen got in the Soviet-Afghan War, but it is enough to keep them fighting, and that is enough to make it a serious problem.

What Can Be Done?

There are a number of possible solutions to the problem of transnational sanctuaries. Counterinsurgent forces can launch all-out invasions of the neighboring countries to clear out sanctuaries. Smaller-scale ground raids or incursions or even air raids or extensive bombing campaigns provide alternative methods for destroying sanctuaries and interdicting supply lines. Counterinsurgent forces also have less direct techniques for dealing with the problem. They can apply diplomatic pressure to neighboring countries, with the hope that the neighbors will police their own borders. They can build barriers made of actual fences or technological sensors along the borders to prevent the entry of insurgents. Some counterinsurgent forces have even tried to resettle the local population away from the borders to help maintain security on the frontier.

The most straightforward options—such as building well-manned barrier systems (as the French did in Algeria) or launching all-out invasions— can be effective. But even these possible solutions have problems. An effective barrier is expensive and requires significant manpower to make it work. And as the French learned, a barrier alone is not enough—counterinsurgent forces still have to win over the civilian population. Full-scale invasions are also problematic—they can lead to a new set of unforeseen problems in the neighboring country.

The historical examples of transnational sanctuaries in irregular warfare indicate that most limited military operations are not effective in denying combatants sanctuary. Airpower, even extensive bombings and attacks such as those used by the Americans in Vietnam, can hinder enemy operations across borders. However, countermeasures, especially antiaircraft fire and ground concealment, have prevented airpower from effectively shutting down borders on its own. The same goes for barrier systems that rely on technology such as mines or sensors to take the place of human patrolling of borders. Sensors and mines may slow cross border activities for as long as it takes the enemy to figure out a way around them, but there has always been a way around the technology. Likewise, ground raids in force across borders can do serious damage to insurgent sanctuaries, but by definition raids are not sustained efforts, and the guerrillas can and do return when the raids end.

So what else can military commanders on the ground do about transnational sanctuaries? The question is a tricky one, because military action along international borders is inevitably constrained by strategies dictated at the highest levels of civilian government. Presidents, cabinet level officials, and even the highest echelons of military command must contend with diplomatic and political concerns that are far outside the purview of the fighting men on the battlefield.[22] Yet barring the construction of an extensive and well-manned barrier systems or all-out invasions, military operations along or across borders must work hand-in-hand with diplomatic and political efforts.

Airpower, technology-driven borders, and raids can be part of a successful effort, but for them to have a lasting effect they require a simultaneous diplomatic effort to convince the bordering nation to police its own side of the border. It is worth noting that there has been little indication that the insurgents have found sanctuary in most of the countries bordering Iraq. Turkey would like nothing more than to keep the border sealed from Kurd-dominated northern Iraq. And although hundreds of Saudi Arabians and dozens of Jordanian nationals have joined the insurgency, the borders with those two countries have remained for the most part secure. There has been little evidence that the guerrillas have active sanctuaries in Jordan or Saudi Arabia.[23] One American military commander responsible for security along the Jordanian border noted, "the Jordanians have a pretty good border. They do a pretty good job controlling the border."[24] The fact that these large sections of Iraq's border are mostly secure suggests that the problem is not intractable. But by far the most effective way to deny insurgents transnational sanctuary—again, short of extensive barriers or all-out invasion—is to convince to neighboring countries to do it themselves.

None of this is to suggest that denying the enemy transnational sanctuaries is some sort of magic bullet for ultimate victory. All of the other hard-learned lessons of counterinsurgency still apply. Counterinsurgent forces must win the trust of the local civilians, they must provide security, and native populations must learn to take control of their own security and their own governance. But denying sanctuaries is an essential, and often overlooked, step to success.

There is a lot of very good advice floating around about how to win in Iraq and Afghanistan. However, with some notable exceptions, most of the contemporary discussions on the situation in Iraq and Afghanistan miss the importance of transnational sanctuary.[25] This is a mistake. In any list of objectives, steps to victory, fundamental principles, or other guides to running successful counterinsurgencies, denying insurgents refuge and supply from outside sources must take a prominent place. Otherwise, the enemy can continue to launch attacks over the border as long as he has the will to do so. In a day and age of the mass media following the mantra of "if it bleeds, it leads," those attacks, no matter how small or insignificant to the overall course of the conflict, dent the confidence and the will of the civilians who support the counterinsurgency forces.

Fanatics, by definition, have the advantage in a battle of wills. Denying them sanctuary means denying them opportunities to wreak havoc. Without those opportunities, even fanatics have no chance.

Endnotes

1. Dale Andrade and James H. Willbanks, "CORDS/Phoenix: Counterinsurgency Lesson from Vietnam for the Future," *Military Review*, 86 (March-April 2006), 9.

2. Many of the studies of the Soviet experience in Afghanistan have focused on other Soviet failures, not denying sanctuary. See, for example, Grau and Nawroz, "Soviet Experience," 26-27, and Stephen D. Pomper, "Don't Follow the Bear: The Soviet Attempt to Build Afghanistan's Military," *Military Review*, 85 (September-October 2005), 26-29.

3. A more comprehensive comparison of the Americans in Vietnam and the Soviets in Afghanistan is Douglas Anthony Borer, "Superpowers Defeated: A Comparison of Vietnam and Afghanistan," (Ph.D. Dissertation, Boston University, 1993).

4. Staniland, "Defeating Transnational Insurgencies," passim; Daniel Byman, et al, *Trends in Outside Support in Insurgent Conflicts* (Santa Monica, CA: RAND, 2001).

5. Peter Paret and John W. Shy, "Guerrilla Warfare and U.S. Military Policy: A Study," *Marine Corps Gazette*, 46 (January 1962), 5.

6. Zasloff, *Role of Sanctuary*, passim. These and other early works on the topic are reviewed in Robertson, "Active Sanctuary," 39-45. Much of this early work was heavily influenced by Mao Zedong's writings on phased guerrilla warfare that envisioned an end game where guerrillas eventually fought larger conventional operations. For some sanctuary only became vitally important in the later phases. See for example, David Galula, *Counterinsurgency Warfare: Theory and Practice* (St. Petersburg, FL: Hailer Publishing, 1964), 39-42; and Robert Thompson, *Defeating Communist Insurgency* (St. Petersburg, FL: Hailer Publishing, 1966), and Robert Thompson, "Squaring the Error," *Foreign Affairs*, 46 (April 1968), 442-453.

7. Christmas, "Guerrilla Sanctuaries," 27.

8. Deiner, "Guerrilla Border Sanctuaries," 176-178.

9. Hamilton, "Defeating Insurgency," passim.

10. Steven Metz, *Counterinsurgency: Strategy and the Phoenix of American Capability* (Carlisle, PA: Strategic Studies Institute, US Army War College, February 1995), 30.

11. Staniland, "Defeating Transnational Insurgencies," 35-37.

12. A general critique of American counterinsurgency doctrine that does not spend much time on sanctuary is Cable, "Reinventing the Round Wheel," passim.

13. Daniel P. Bolger, *Scenes from an Unfinished War: Low-Intensity Conflict in Korea, 1966-1969*, Leavenworth Paper No. 19, (Fort Leavenworth, KS: Combat Studies Institute, 1991), 44-45.

14. FM 31-10, *Denial Operations*, passim.

15. United States Department of the Army, FM 90-8, *Counterguerrilla Operations* (Washington, DC: GPO, August 1986), 3-44-3-47.

16. The manual on support operations notes in an appendix that external support is often a key aspect of insurgencies, but does not offer suggestions on how to cut off that support. FM 3-07, *Stability Operations and Support Operations* (Washington, DC: GPO, February 2003), D-6. The manual on counterinsurgency operations also cites external support for insurgents but provides no guidance on how to cut off such support. FM 3-07.22, *Counterinsurgency Operations* (Washington, DC: GPO, October 2004), 1-8.

17. Nadav Hillebrand, "Afghan Hound," *Jerusalem Report*, (2 June 2003), 32.

18. Fighting continues in Afghanistan, but other concerns are starting to take precedence, for example the renewed opiate growing market. Although there is growing concern about terrorist efforts in the southwest, across from Baluchistan in Pakistan. See, for example, Shawn Brimley, "Tentacles of Jihad: Targeting Transnational Support Networks," *Parameters*, 36 (Summer 2006), 30-46; Ann Scott Tyson, "Afghan Threat Played Down; NATO Chief Says Revived Insurgency Isn't Likely," *Washington Post*, 7 March 2006, A13; Richard Holbrooke, "Afghanistan: The Long Road Ahead," *Washington Post*, 2 April 2006, B7; "U.S. Sponsors Seminar for Afghanistan-Pakistan Border Security," 3 April 2006; and Mirwais Afghan, "US-led attack kills 76 in Afghanistan," *Washington Post*, 22 May 2006.

19. Some observers question whether what is going on in Iraq can even properly be called an "insurgency." For example, Ian Beckett writes, "there is not yet the cohesive leadership, political vision, strategic direction, or unifying ideology to suggest the emergence of a real insurgency.... The situation in Iraq has been characterized as perhaps an example of a 'net war', in which loose groups often diametrically opposed to one another gravitate towards one another to carry out attacks, trade weapons or intelligence, and disperse, never to cooperate again." Ian F.W. Beckett, *Insurgency in Iraq: An Historical Perspective* (Carlisle, PA: Strategic Studies Institute, U.S. Army War College, January 2005), 5-6.

20. Of course, all is not perfect: one area in particular where the lessons took longer to recall was convoy security. Improvised explosive devices have provided the greatest new challenge.

21. Joshua Green, "The Numbers War," *Atlantic Monthly*, 297 (May 2006), 36-37; Michael E. O'Hanlon and Nina Kamp, "Iraq Index," 18 May 2006, Brookings Institution, Online: http://www.brookings.edu/iraqindex, 4-19.

22. The problem is exacerbated by the American military's traditional tendency to look at civilian leadership as amateurish and dangerously restrictive when it comes to military affairs. For a primer on military distrust of civilian leadership, see Russell F. Weigley, "The Soldier, the Statesman, and the Military Historian," *Journal of Military History*, 63 (October 1999), 807-822.

23. O'Hanlon and Kamp, "Iraq Index," 19. Jordan was an ally in the initial invasion of Iraq, allowing Special Forces to operate from Jordanian territory. Saudi Arabia has been neutral, but Special Forces also used Saudi territory. Recently the Saudis even began toying with the idea of sealing their own border with Iraq to keep *out* the violence. See Woodward, *Plan of Attack*, 257-264, 353-354; Franks, *American Soldier*, 404-406; "Marines Keep Watchful Eye on Iraq's Rural Western Region," *US Federal News Service*, 29 March 2006; Rasheed Abou-Alsamh, "Saudis Mull Electric Fence on Iraqi Border," *Christian Science Monitor*, 20 April 2006, 7.

24. Teeples interview.

25. For example see Robert M. Cassidy, *Counterinsurgency and the Global War on Terror* (Westport, CT: Praeger, 2006); Andrew F. Krepinevich, "How to Win in Iraq," *Foreign Affairs*, 84 (September-October 2005), 87-99; Bruce Hoffman, *Insurgency and Counterinsurgency in Iraq* (Santa Monica, CA: RAND, June 2004); David Voorhies, "Stability Operations: The Legacy of Search and Attack," *Infantry*, 94 (May-June 2005), 27-34; Frederick W. Kagan, "A Plan for Victory in Iraq," *Weekly Standard*, 11 (29 May 2006); "How to Do Better," *Economist*, 14 December 2005, Online: http://www.economist.com, (accessed 1 February 2006); Thomas E. Ricks, "The Lessons of Counterinsurgency," *Washington Post*, 16 February 2006, A14; Robert D. Kaplan, "The Coming Normalcy?" *Atlantic Monthly*, 297 (April 2006), 72-81; Andrade and Willbanks, "CORDS/Phoenix," 22; and Beckett, *Insurgency in Iraq*, passim. Studies that have focused on the sanctuary question the in war on terror but disagree on how to deal with it include Staniland, "Defeating Transnational Insurgencies," passim; Brimley, "Tentacles of Jihad," 40-43; Colin S. Gray, *Irregular Enemies and the Essence of Strategy: Can the American Way of War Adapt?* (Carlisle, PA: Strategic Studies Institute, US Army War College, March 2006), 26; and John A. Lynn, "Patterns of Insurgency and Counterinsurgency," *Military Review*, 85 (July-August 2005), 22-27.

BIBLIOGRAPHY

Archives and Primary Sources:

"After Action Report, Ia Drang Valley Operation, 1st Battalion, 7th Cavalry." 9 December 1965. In author's possession.

Central Intelligence Agency, Freedom of Information Act Electronic Reading Room. Online: http://www.foia.cia.gov.

Cold War International History Project. Woodrow Wilson International Center for Scholars. Online: www.wilsoncenter.org.

Foreign Relations of the United States: Vietnam, 1964, vol. I. Washington DC: GPO, 1992.

Jimmy Carter Presidential Library. Online: http://www.jimmycarterlibrary.gov.

Naftali, Timothy and Philip Zelikow, eds. *The Presidential Recordings: John F. Kennedy, The Great Crises, Volume Two.* New York: W.W. Norton, 2001.

National Security Archive. Afghanistan: The Making of U.S. Policy, 1973-1990. Microfiche. Alexandria, VA: Chadwyck-Healey, 1990.

_____. George Washington University, Online: http://www.gwu.edu/~nsarchiv.

Office of the Deputy Chief of Staff for Military Operations. *A Program for the Pacification and Long-Term Development of South Vietnam*, 2 vols. Department of the Army, 1966.

O'Hanlon, Michael E. and Nina Kamp. "Iraq Index." Brookings Institution. Online: www.brookings.edu/iraqindex.

Public Papers of the Presidents, The American Presidency Project, Online: http://www.presidency.ucsb.edu.

The Pentagon Papers (Gravel Edition), 5 vols. Boston: Beacon Press, 1971-1972.

Ronald Reagan Presidential Library. Online: http://www.reagan.utexas.edu.

United States Congress, Senate Armed Forces Committee. *Report of the Electronic Battlefield Program. 92d Congress, 1st Session.* Washington, DC: GPO, 1971.

Virtual Vietnam Archive. Texas Tech University. Online: http://www.vietnam.ttu.edu.

Doctrinal Publications

United States Department of the Army. FM 3-07. *Stability Operations and Support Operations*. Washington, DC: GPO, February 2003.

United States Department of the Army. FM 3-07.22. *Counterinsurgency Operations*. Washington, DC: GPO, October 2004.

United States Department of the Army. FM 31-55. *Border Security/Anti-Infiltration Operations*. Washington, DC: GPO, March 1972.

United States Department of the Army. FM 31-10. *Denial Operations and Barriers* Washington, DC: GPO, September 1968.

United States Department of the Army. FM 90-8. *Counterguerrilla Operations* Washington, DC: GPO, August 1986.

United States Marine Corps. *Small Wars Manual – 1940*. Washington, DC: GPO, 1940.

Books and Short Studies

Alexiev, Alexander. *The United States and the War in Afghanistan*. Santa Monica, CA: RAND, 1988.

Amstutz, J. Bruce. *Afghanistan: The First Five Years of Soviet Occupation*. Washington, DC: National Defense University Press, 1986.

Andrade, Dale. *America's Last Vietnam Battle: Halting Hanoi's 1972 Easter Offensive*. Lawrence: University Press of Kansas, 2001.

_____. *Ashes to Ashes: The Phoenix Program and the Vietnam War*. Lexington, MA: Lexington Books, 1990.

Andrew, Christopher. *For the President's Eyes Only: Secret Intelligence and the American Presidency from Washington to Bush*. New York: HarperCollins, 1995.

_____. and Oleg Gordievsky. *KGB: The Inside Story*. New York: HarperCollins, 1990.

_____. and Vasili Mitrokin. *The World Was Going Our Way: The KGB and the Battle for the Third World*. New York: Basic Books, 2005.

Appy, Christian G. *Patriots: The Vietnam War Remembered from All Sides*. New York: Viking, 2003.

Arnold, Anthony. *The Fateful Pebble: Afghanistan's Role in the Fall of the Soviet Empire*. Novato, CA: Presidio Press, 1993.

Ballard, Jack S. *Development and Employment of Fixed Wing Gunships, 1962-1972*. Washington, DC: Office of Air Force History, 1982.

Baumann, Robert F. *Russian-Soviet Unconventional Wars in the Caucasus, Central Asia, and Afghanistan*. Leavenworth Paper Number 20. Fort Leavenworth, KS: Combat Studies Institute, 1993.

Beardon, Milt and James Rosen. *The Main Enemy: The Inside Story of the CIA's Final Showdown with the KGB*. New York: Random House, 2003.

Beckett, Ian F.W. *Insurgency in Iraq: An Historical Perspective*. Carlisle, PA: Strategic Studies Institute. U.S. Army War College, January 2005.

Bickel, Keith B. *Mars Learning: The Marine Corps Development of Small Wars Doctrine, 1915-1940*. Boulder, CO: Westview Press, 2001.

Birtle, Andrew J. *U.S. Army Counterinsurgency and Contingency Operations Doctrine*. Washington, DC: US Army Center of Military History, 2004.

Blood and Steel!: The History, Customs, and Traditions of the 3d Armored Cavalry Regiments. Fort Carson, CO: Third Cavalry Museum, n.d.

Bolger, Daniel P. *Scenes from an Unfinished War: Low-Intensity Conflict in Korea, 1966-1969*. Leavenworth Paper No. 19. Fort Leavenworth, KS: Combat Studies Institute, 1991.

Boot, Max. *The Savage Wars of Peace: Small Wars and the Rise of American Power*. New York: Basic Books, 2002.

Bremer, L. Paul. *My Year in Iraq: The Struggle to Build a Future of Hope*. New York: Simon and Schuster, 2006.

Brownlee, W. Eliot and Hugh Davis Graham, eds. *The Reagan Presidency: Pragmatic Conservatism and Its Legacies*. Lawrence: University Press of Kansas, 2003.

Brzezinski, Zbigniew. *Power and Principle: Memoirs of the National Security Advisor, 1977-1981*. New York: Farrar Straus Giroux, 1983.

Byman, Daniel, et al. *Trends in Outside Support in Insurgent Conflicts*. Santa Monica, CA: RAND, 2001.

Cannon, Lou. *President Reagan: The Role of a Lifetime*. New York: Simon and Schuster, 1991.

Carter, Jimmy. *Keeping Faith: Memoirs of a President*. Toronto: Bantam Books, 1982.

Clarke, Jeffrey J. *Advice and Support: The Final Years, 1965-1973*. Washington, DC: Center of Military History, 1988.

Cassidy, Robert M. *Counterinsurgency and the Global War on Terror*. Westport, CT: Praeger, 2006.

Clodfelter, Mark. *The Limits of Airpower: The American Bombing of North Vietnam*. New York: Free Press, 1989.

Coleman, J.D. *Incursion: From America's Chokehold on the NVA Lifelines to the Sacking of the Cambodian Sanctuaries*. New York: St. Martin's Paperbacks, 1991.

Conboy, Kenneth. *Shadow War: The CIA's Secret War in Laos*. Boulder, CO: Paladin Press, 1995.

Cordovez, Diego and Selig S. Harrison. *Out of Afghanistan: The Inside Story of the Soviet Withdrawal*. New York: Oxford University Press, 1995.

Cosmas, Graham A. and Terrence P. Murray. *U.S. Marines in Vietnam: Vietnamization and Redeployment, 1970-1971*. Washington, DC: USMC History and Museums Division, 1986.

Currey, Cecil B. *Edward Lansdale: The Unquiet American*. Boston: Houghton Mifflin, 1988.

Daugherty, William J. *Executive Secrets: Covert Action and the Presidency*. Lexington: University Press of Kentucky, 2004.

Davidson, Philip B. *Vietnam at War: The History: 1946-1975*. Novato, CA: Presidio Press, 1988.

Dickson, Paul. *The Electronic Battlefield*. Bloomington: Indiana University Press, 1976.

Dorronsoro, Gilles. *Revolution Unending: Afghanistan: 1979 to the Present*. New York: Columbia University Press, 2005.

Duiker, William J. *Sacred War: Nationalism and Revolution in a Divided Vietnam*. New York: McGraw Hill, 1995.

Eliot, Theodore L. and Robert L. Pfaltzgraff, eds. *The Red Army on Pakistan's Border: Policy Implications for the United States*. Washington, DC: Pergamon-Brassey's, 1986.

Fall, Bernard B. *Hell in a Very Small Place: The Siege of Dien Bien Phu*. New York: De Capo Press, 1966.

_____. *Street Without Joy*. Harrisburg, PA: Stackpole Books, 1967.

Farr, Grant M. and John G. Merriam, eds. *Afghan Resistance: The Politics of Survival*. Boulder, CO: Westview Press, 1987.

Fink, Gary M. and Hugh Davis Graham, eds. *The Carter Presidency: Policy Choices in the Post-New Deal Era*. Lawrence: University Press of Kansas, 1999.

FitzGerald, Frances. *Fire in the Lake: The Vietnamese and Americans in Vietnam*. New York: Random House, 1983.

Fontenot, Gregory, et al. *On Point: The United States Army in Operation Iraqi Freedom*. Fort Leavenworth, KS: Combat Studies Institute Press, 2004.

Fox, Roger P. *Air Base Defense in the Republic of Vietnam, 1961-1973*. Washington, DC: Office of Air Force History, 1979.

Franks, Tommy. *American Soldier*. New York: HarperCollins, 2004.

Galeotti, Mark. *Afghanistan: The Soviet Union's Last War*. London: Frank Cass, 1995.

Galula, David. *Counterinsurgency Warfare: Theory and Practice*. St. Petersburg, FL: Hailer Publishing, 1964.

Gates, Robert M. *From the Shadows: The Ultimate Insider's Story of Five Presidents and How They Won the Cold War*. New York: Simon and Schuster, 1996.

Gilbert, Marc Jason, and William Head, eds. *The Tet Offensive*. Westport, CT: Praeger, 1996.

Gilster, Herman L. *The Air War in Southeast Asia: Case Studies of Selected Campaigns*. Maxwell Air Force Base, AL: Air University Press, 1993.

Girardet, Edward. *Afghanistan: The Soviet War*. New York: St. Martin's Press, 1985.

Gordon, Michael R. and Bernard E. Trainor. *COBRA II: The Inside Story of the Invasion and Occupation of Iraq*. New York: Pantheon Books, 2006.

Grau, Lester W., ed. *The Bear Went Over the Mountain: Soviet Combat Tactics in Afghanistan*. Washington, DC: National Defense University Press, 1996.

Gray, Colin S. *Irregular Enemies and the Essence of Strategy: Can the American Way of War Adapt?* Carlisle, PA: Strategic Studies Institute, US Army War College, March 2006.

Greenberg, Lawrence M. *The Hukbalahap Insurrection: A Case Study of a Successful Anti-Insurgency Operation in the Philippines – 1946-1955*. Washington, DC: U.S. Army Center of Military History, 1986.

Haas, Michael E. *Apollo's Warriors: United States Air Force Special Operations during the Cold War*. Maxwell Air Force Base, Alabama: Air University Press, 1997.

Hammond, Thomas T. *Red Flag Over Afghanistan: The Communist Coup, the Soviet Invasion, and the Consequences*. Boulder, CO: Westview Press, 1984.

Hannah, Norman B. *The Key to Failure: Laos and the Vietnam War*. Lanham, MD: Madison Books, 1987.

Herring, George C. *America's Longest War: The United States and Vietnam, 1950-1975*, 3d ed. New York: McGraw Hill, 1996.

Hinh, Nguyen Duy. *Lam Son 719*. Washington, DC: Center of Military History, 1979.

Hoffman, Bruce. *Insurgency and Counterinsurgency in Iraq*. Santa Monica, CA: RAND, June 2004.

Huber, Thomas M., ed. *Compound Warfare: That Fatal Knot*. Fort Leavenworth, KS: U.S. Army Command and General Staff College Press, 2002.

Hunt, Richard A. *Pacification: The American Struggle for Vietnam's Hearts and Minds*. Boulder, CO: Westview Press, 1995.

Jalali, Ali Ahmad and Lester W. Grau, eds. *Afghan Guerilla Warfare: In the Words of the Mujahideen Fighters*. London: Compendium, 2001.

Joes, Anthony James. *America and Guerilla Warfare*. Lexington: University Press of Kentucky, 2000.

Kakar, M. Hassan. *Afghanistan: The Soviet Invasion and the Afghan Response, 1979-1982*. Berkeley: University of California Press, 1995.

Karnow, Stanley. *Vietnam: A History*. New York: Viking, 1983.

Kaufman, Burton I. *The Presidency of James Earl Carter, Jr.* Lawrence: University Press of Kansas, 1993.

Kelly, Francis J. *U.S. Army Special Forces*, Vietnam Studies. Washington, DC: Center of Military History, 1973.

Khan, Riaz M. *Untying the Afghan Knot: Negotiating Soviet Withdrawal*. Durham, NC: Duke University Press, 1991.

Kinnard, Douglas. *The Certain Trumpet: Maxwell Taylor and the American Experience in Vietnam*. Washington, DC: Brassey's, 1991.

Komer, Robert W. *Impact of Pacification on Insurgency in South Vietnam*. Santa Monica, CA: RAND, 1970.

Krepinevich, Andrew F. *The Army and Vietnam*. Baltimore, MD: Johns Hopkins University Press, 1986.

Kuzichkin, Vladimir. *Inside the KGB: My Life in Soviet Espionage*. New York: Pantheon Books, 1990.

Laber, Jeri and Barnett R. Rubin. *"A Nation is Dying": Afghanistan Under the Soviets, 1979-87*. Evanston, IL: Northwestern University Press, 1988.

Lanning, Michael Lee, and Dan Cragg. *Inside the VC and the NVA*. New York: Ivy Books, 1992.

Lavalle, A.J.C., ed. *Airpower and the 1972 Spring Invasion*. Washington, DC: Office of Air Force History, 1985.

Le Gro, William E. *Vietnam from Cease-Fire to Capitulation*. Washington, DC: U.S. Army Center of Military History, 1985.

Lewy, Guenter. *America in Vietnam*. New York: Oxford University Press, 1978.

Logevall, Frederik. *Choosing War: The Lost Chance for Peace and the Escalation of War in Vietnam*. Berkeley: University of California Press, 1999.

Lohbeck, Kurt. *Holy War, Unholy Victory: Eyewitness to the CIA's Secret War in Afghanistan*. Washington, DC: Regnery, 1993.

MacEachin, Douglas J. *Predicting the Soviet Invasion of Afghanistan: The Intelligence Community's Record*. Washington, DC: Center for the Study of Intelligence, 2002.

McMichael, Scott R. *Stumbling Bear: Soviet Military Performance in Afghanistan*. London: Brassey's, 1991.

Metz, Steven. *Counterinsurgency: Strategy and the Phoenix of American Capability*. Carlisle, PA: Strategic Studies Institute. US Army War College, February 1995.

Metzner, Edward P. *More Than a Soldier's War: Pacification in Vietnam*. College Station: Texas A&M University Press, 1995.

Mitrokin, Vasiliy. *The KGB in Afghanistan*. Working Paper No. 40. Washington, DC: Cold War International History Project, 2002.

Moore Harold G. and Joseph L. Galloway. *We Were Soldiers Once...And Young*. New York: Random House, 1992.

Momyer, William M. *Airpower in Three Wars*. Maxwell Air Force Base, AL: Air University Press, 2003.

Moyar, Mark. *Phoenix and the Birds of Prey: The CIA's Secret Campaign to Destroy the Viet Cong*. Annapolis, MD: Naval Institute Press, 1997.

Nalty, Bernard C. *Airpower and the Fight for Khe Sanh*. Washington, DC: Office of Air Force History, 1986.

_____. *The War Against the Trucks: Aerial Interdiction in Southern Laos*. Washington, DC: Air Force History and Museums Program, 2005.

Nolan, Keith W. *Into Cambodia: Spring Campaign, Summer Offensive, 1970*. Novato, CA: Presidio Press, 1990.

_____. *Into Laos: the Story of Dewey Canyon II/Lam Son 719; Vietnam 1971*. Novato, CA: Presidio Press, 1986.

Oberdorfer, Don. *Tet!* Garden City, NY: Doubleday, 1971.

_____. *The Turn: From the Cold War to a New Era*. New York: Poseidon Press, 1991.

Palmer, Bruce. *The 25-Year War*. Lexington: University Press of Kentucky, 1984.

Pike, Douglas. *PAVN: People's Army of Vietnam*. Novato, CA: Presidio Press, 1986.

Pisor, Robert L. *The End of the Line: The Siege of Khe Sanh*. New York: Norton, 1982.

Plaster, John L. *SOG: The Secret Wars of America's Commandos in Vietnam*. New York: Simon and Schuster, 1997.

Prados, John. The Blood Road: The Ho Chi Minh Trail and the Vietnam War. New York: John Wiley and Sons, 1999.

_____, and Ray William Stubbe. *Valley of Decision: The Siege of Khe Sanh*. Boston: Houghton Mifflin, 1991.

Richelson, Jeffrey. *The U.S. Intelligence Community*. 2d edition. Cambridge, MA: Ballinger Publishing, 1989.

Robbins, Christopher. *The Ravens: The Men Who Flew in America's Secret War in Laos*. New York: Crown Publishers, 1987.

Rosenau, William. *Special Operations Forces and Elusive Enemy Ground Targets: Lessons from Vietnam and the Persian Gulf War*. Santa Monica, CA: RAND, 2001.

Roy, Olivier. *Afghanistan: From Holy War to Civil War*. Princeton, NJ: Darwin Press, 1995.

_____. *Islam and Resistance in Afghanistan*. 2d edition. Cambridge University Press, 1990.

Rubin, Barnett R. *The Search for Peace in Afghanistan: From Buffer State to Failed State*. New Haven, CT: Yale University Press, 1995.

Sada, Georges. *Saddam's Secrets: How an Iraqi General Defied and Survived Saddam Hussein*. Nashville, TN: Integrity Publishers, 2006.

Saikal, Amin. *Modern Afghanistan: A History of Struggle and Survival*. London: I.B. Tauris, 2004.

_____. and William Maley, eds. *The Soviet Withdrawal from Afghanistan*. Cambridge University Press, 1989.

Sarin, Oleg and Lev Dvoretsky. *The Afghan Syndrome: The Soviet Union's Vietnam*. Novato, CA: Presidio Press, 1993.

Sarkesian, Sam C. *America's Forgotten Wars: The Counterrevolutionary Past and Lessons for the Future*. Westport, CT: Greenwood Press, 1984.

Schweizer, Peter. *Reagan's War: The Epic Story of His Forty-Year Struggle and Final Triumph Over Communism*. New York: Doubleday, 2002.

Scoville, Thomas W. *Reorganizing for Pacification Support*. Washington, DC: Center of Military History, 1982.

Sharp, U.S. Grant. *Strategy for Defeat: Vietnam in Retrospect*. San Rafael, CA: Presidio Press, 1978.

Shaw, John M. *The Cambodian Campaign: The 1970 Offensive and America's Vietnam War*. Lawrence: University Press of Kansas, 2005.

Sheehan, Neil. *A Bright Shining Lie: John Paul Vann and America in Vietnam*. New York: Random House, 1988.

Shultz, George P. *Turmoil and Triumph: My Years as Secretary of State*. New York: Charles Scribner's Sons, 1993.

Simpson, Charles M. *Inside the Green Berets: The First Thirty Years*. Novato, CA: Presidio Press, 1983.

Smith, Gaddis. *Morality, Reason, and Power: American Diplomacy in the Carter Years*. New York: Hill and Wang, 1986.

Sorley, Lewis. *A Better War: The Unexamined Victories and Final Tragedy of America's Last Years in Vietnam*. New York: Harcourt Brace, 1999.

_____. *Honorable Warrior: General Harold K. Johnson and the Ethics of Command*. Lawrence: University Press of Kansas, 1998.

_____. ed. *Vietnam Chronicles: The Abrams Tapes, 1968-1972*. Lubbock: Texas Tech University Press, 2004.

Spector, Ronald H. Advice and Support: The Early Years, 1941-1960. Washington DC: Center of Military History, 1983.

_____. *After Tet: The Bloodiest Year in Vietnam*. New York: Free Press, 1993.

Stanton, Shelby L. *Green Berets at War: U.S. Army Special Forces in Southeast Asia, 1956-1975*. Novato, CA: Presidio Press, 1985.

Stewart, Richard W. *The United States Army in Afghanistan: Operation Enduring Freedom*. Washington, DC: US Army Center of Military History, n.d.

Summers, Harry G. *On Strategy: The Vietnam War in Context*. Carlisle Barracks, PA: Strategic Studies Institute, 1982.

Tang, Troung Nhu. *A Vietcong Memoir*. San Diego, CA: Harcourt Brace Jovanovich, 1985.

Tanner, Stephen. *Afghanistan: A Military History from Alexander the Great to the Fall of the Taliban*. New York: Da Capo Press, 2002.

Taylor, Maxwell D. *Swords and Plowshares*. New York: W.W. Norton, 1972.

Taylor, John M. *General Maxwell Taylor: The Sword and the Pen*. New York: Doubleday, 1989.

Telfer, Gary L. et al. *U.S. Marines in Vietnam: Fighting the North Vietnamese, 1967*. Washington, DC: USMC History and Museums Division, 1984.

Thi, Lam Quang. *The Twenty-Five Year Century: A South Vietnamese General Remembers the Indochina War to the Fall of Saigon*. Denton: University of North Texas Press, 2001.

Tho, Tran Dinh. *The Cambodian Incursion*. Washington, DC: Center of Military History, 1980.

_____. *Pacification*. Washington, DC: Center of Military History, 1980.

Thompson, Robert. *Defeating Communist Insurgency*. St. Petersburg, FL: Hailer Publishing, 1966.

Tilford, Earl H. *Crosswinds: The Air Force's Setup in Vietnam*. College Station: Texas A&M University Press, 1993.

Truong, Ngo Quang. *The Easter Offensive of 1972*. Washington, DC: U.S. Army Center of Military History, 1980.

Urban, Mark. *War in Afghanistan*. New York: St. Martin's Press, 1988.

Van Staaveren, Jacob. *Interdiction in Southern Laos, 1960-1968*. Washington, DC: Center for Air Force History, 1993.

Westmoreland, William C. *A Soldier Reports*. Garden City, NY: Doubleday, 1976.

Willbanks, James H. *Abandoning Vietnam: How America Left and South Vietnam Lost Its War*. Lawrence: University Press of Kansas, 2004.

_____. *The Battle of An Loc*. Bloomington: University of Indiana Press, 2005.

_____. *Thiet Giap! The Battle of An Loc*. Fort Leavenworth, KS: Combat Studies Institute Press, 1993.

Woodward, Bob. *Plan of Attack*. New York: Simon and Schuster, 2004.

Yousaf, Mohammad and Mark Adkin. *Afghanistan—The Bear Trap: The Defeat of a Superpower*. Havertown, PA: Casemate, 2001.

Zasloff, Joseph Jeremiah. *The Role of Sanctuary in Insurgency: Communist China's Support to the Vietminh, 1946-1954*. Santa Monica, CA: RAND, 1967.

Articles and Papers

Amin, Tahir. "Afghan Resistance: Past, Present, and Future." *Asian Survey*. 24 (April 1984); 373-399.

Andrade, Dale. "Crossing the Line: Assault Into Cambodia." *Military History Quarterly*. 13 (Winter 2001): 22-29.

_____, and James H. Willbanks. "CORDS/Phoenix: Counterinsurgency Lesson from Vietnam for the Future." *Military Review*. 86 (March-April 2006): 9-23.

August, Melissa. "Cozying Up To Syria." *Time*. 164 (27 September 2004): 17.

Bennigsen, Alexandre. "Mullahs, Mujahidin and Soviet Muslims." *Problems of Communism*. 33 (November-December 1984): 28-44.

Biggio, Charles P. "Let's Learn From the French." *Military Review*. 46 (October 1966): 27-34.

Black, Edwin F. "Advisory Warfare vs. Sanctuary Warfare." *U.S. Naval Institute Proceedings*. 91 (February 1965): 34-42.

Brigham, Erwin R. "Pacification Measurement." *Military Review*. 50 (May 1970): 47-55.

Brimley, Shawn. "Tentacles of Jihad: Targeting Transnational Support Networks." *Parameters*. 36 (Summer 2006): 30-46.

Brower, Charles F. "Strategic Reassessment in Vietnam: The Westmoreland 'Alternate Strategy' of 1967-1968." *Naval War College Review*. 44 (Spring 1991): 20-51.

Brush, Peter W. "The Significance of Local Communist Forces In Post-Tet Vietnam." Online: www.library.vanderbilt.edu/central/brush/LocalForces.htm. accessed 27 February 2006.

_____. "The Story Behind the McNamara Line." *Vietnam* (February 1996): 18-24.

Cable, Larry. "Reinventing the Round Wheel: Insurgency, Counter-Insurgency, and Peacekeeping Post Cold War." *Small Wars and Insurgencies*. 4 (Autumn 1993): 228-262.

Cassidy, Robert M. "Back to the Street Without Joy: Counterinsurgency Lessons from Vietnam and Other Small Wars." *Parameters*, 34 (Summer 2004): 73-83.

Cash, John A. "Fight at the Ia Drang." in *Seven Firefights in Vietnam*. eds. John A. Cash, John Albright, and Allan W. Sandstrum. Washington, DC: Center of Military History, 1985.

Chen Jian, "China's Involvement in the Vietnam War, 1964-1969." *China Quarterly*. 142 (June 1995): 356-387.

Christmas, G.R. "Guerrilla Sanctuaries." *Infantry*. 63 (May-June 1973): 24-27.

Cochran, Alexander S. "American Planning for Ground Combat in Vietnam, 1952-1965." *Parameters*. 14 (Summer 1984): 63-69.

Cogan, Charles G. "Partners in Time: The CIA and Afghanistan since 1979." *World Policy Journal*. 10 (Summer 1993): 73-82.

Cohen, Stephen P. "South Asia After Afghanistan." *Problems of Communism*. 34 (January-February 1985): 18-31.

Coldren, Lee O. "Afghanistan in 1985: The Sixth Year of the Russo-Afghan War." *Asian Survey*. 26 (February 1986): 235-245.

Correll, John T. "The Ho Chi Minh Trail." *Air Force Magazine*. 88 (November 2005): 62-68.

Daley, Ted. "Afghanistan and Gorbachev's Global Foreign Policy." *Asian Survey*. 29 (May 1989): 496-513.

Deiner, John D. "Guerrilla Border Sanctuaries and Counterinsurgent Warfare." *Army Quarterly and Defense Journal*. 109 (April 1979): 162-179.

Dickson, Keith D. "The Basmachi and the Mujahidin: Soviet Responses to Insurgency Movements." *Military Review*. 65 (February 1985): 29-44.

Drew, Dennis M. "U.S. Airpower Theory and the Insurgent Challenge." *Journal of Military History*. 62 (October 1998): 809-832.

Dunbar, Charles. "Afghanistan in 1986: The Balance Endures." *Asian Survey*. 27 (February 1987):127-142.

Dupree, Nancy Hatch. "Demographic Reporting on Afghan Refugees in Pakistan." *Modern Asian Studies*. 22 (1988): 845-865.

Eliot, Theodore L. "Afghanistan in 1989: Stalemate." *Asian Survey*. 30 (February 1990): 158-166.

Fang, Bay. "Keeping an Eye on the Exit." *U.S. News and World Report*. 134 (12 May 2003): 19.

Fulbrook, Jim E. "Lam Son 719: Part I: Prelude to Air Assault." *U.S. Army Aviation Digest*. 32 (June 1986): 2-15.

_____. "Lam Son 719: Part II: The Battle." *U.S. Army Aviation Digest*. 32 (July 1986): 34-45.

_____. "Lam Son 719: Part III: Reflections and Values." *U.S. Army Aviation Digest*. 32 (August 1986): 3-13.

Gaiduk, Ilya V. "The Vietnam War and Soviet-American Relations, 1964-1973: New Russian Evidence." *Cold War International History Project Bulletin*. 6-7 (Winter 1995-1996): 231, 250-257.

Gates, John M. "People's War in Vietnam." *Journal of Military History*. 54 (July 1990): 325-344.

Gibbs, David. "Does the USSR Have a 'Grand Strategy'? Reinterpreting the Invasion of Afghanistan." *Journal of Peace Research*. 24 (December 1987): 365-379.

Gole, Henry G. "Shadow Wars and Secret Wars: Phoenix and MACVSOG." *Parameters*. 21 (Winter 1991-92): 95-105.

Grau Lester W. and Mohammand Yahya Nawroz. "The Soviet Experience in Afghanistan." *Military Review*. 75 (September-October 1995): 16-27.

Greeley, Richard S. "Stringing the McNamara Line," *Naval History*, 11 (July/August 1997): 60-66.

Green, Joshua. "The Numbers War." *Atlantic Monthly*. 297 (May 2006): 36-37.

Herring, George C. "The 1st Cavalry and the Ia Drang Valley, 18 October-24 November 1965," in *America's First Battles, 1776-1965*. eds. Charles E. Heller and William A. Stofft. Lawrence: University Press of Kansas, 1986.

Herrmann, Richard K. "Soviet Behavior in Regional Conflicts: Old Questions, New Strategies, and Important Lessons." *World Politics*. 44 (April 1992): 432-465.

Hillebrand, Nadav. "Afghan Hound," *Jerusalem Report*. (2 June 2003): 32. "How to Do Better." *Economist*. 14 December 2005. Online: www.economist.com accessed 1 February 2006.

Jones, Frank L. "Blowtorch: Robert Komer and the Making of Vietnam Pacification Policy." *Parameters*. 35 (Autumn 2005): 103-118.

Kagan, Frederick W. "A Plan for Victory in Iraq." *Weekly Standard*. 11 (29 May 2006).

Kaplan, Robert D. "The Coming Normalcy?" *Atlantic Monthly*. 297 (April 2006): 72-81.

Karp, Aaron. "Blowpipes and Stingers in Afghanistan: One Year Later." *Armed Forces Journal International*. 125 (September 1987): 36-40.

Khalilzad, Zalmay. "Moscow's Afghan War." Problems of Communism. 35 (January-February 1986): 1-20.

_____. "Soviet-Occupied Afghanistan." *Problems of Communism*. 29 (Nov-Dec 1980): 23-40.

Kolb, Richard K. "Hitting the Ho Chi Minh Trail." *VFW, Veterans of Foreign Wars Magazine*. 83 (February 1996): 33-38.

Kopets, Keith F. "The Combined Action Program: Vietnam." *Military Review*. 82 (July-August 2002): 78-81.

Krepinevich, Andrew F. "How to Win in Iraq." *Foreign Affairs*. 84 (September-October 2005): 87-99.

Kuperman, Alan J. "The Stinger Missile and U.S. Intervention in Afghanistan." *Political Science Quarterly*. 114 (Summer 1999): 219-263.

Linn, Brian McAllister. "The Impact of the Imperial Wars (1898-1907) on the US Army." *Heritage Lectures*. 908 (14 November 2005): 1-10.

Lomperis, Timothy J. "Giap's Dream, Westmoreland's Nightmare." *Parameters*. 18 (June 1988): 18-32.

Lynn, John A. "Patterns of Insurgency and Counterinsurgency." *Military Review*. 85 (July-August 2005): 22-27.

McCormick, Kip. "The Evolution of Soviet Military Doctrine, Afghanistan." *Military Review*. 67 (July 1987): 61-72.

McGeary, Johanna. "The Trouble With Syria." *Time*. 165 (28 February 2005): 30-31.

Meadows, Michael V. "Into the Lion's Den." *Vietnam*. (August 2005): 18-24.

Mecham, Michael. "U.S. Credits Afghan Resistance with Thwarting Soviet Air-power." *Aviation Week and Space Technology*. 127 (13 July 1987): 26-27.

Mendelson, Sarah E. "Internal Battles and External Wars: Politics, Learning, and the Soviet Withdrawal from Afghanistan." *World Politics*. 45 (April 1993): 327-360.

O'Ballance, Edgar. "The Ho Chi Minh Trail." *Army Quarterly and Defense Journal*. 94 (April 1967): 105-110.

_____. "Pakistan: On the Front Porch of Conflict." *Military Review*. 66 (March 1986): 68-75.

_____. "Soviet Tactics in Afghanistan." *Military Review*. 60 (August 1980): 45-52.

Paret, Peter, and John W. Shy. "Guerrilla Warfare and U.S. Military Policy: A Study." *Marine Corps Gazette*. 46 (January 1962): 1-8.

Paul, T.V. "Influence Through Arms Transfers: Lessons from the U.S.-Pakistani Relationship." *Asian Survey*. 32 (December 1992): 1078-1092.

Payind, Alam. "Soviet-Afghan Relations from Cooperation to Occupation." *International Journal of Middle East Studies*. 21 (February 1989): 107-128.

Pomper, Stephen D. "Don't Follow the Bear: The Soviet Attempt to Build Afghanistan's Military." *Military Review*. 85 (September-October 2005): 26-29.

Possony, Stefan T. "Battle, No Longer the Payoff?" *U.S. Naval Institute Proceedings*. 96 (September 1970): 33-37.

Qiang Zhai. "Beijing and the Vietnam Conflict, 1964-1965: New Chinese Evidence." *Cold War International History Project Bulletin.* 6-7 (Winter 1995-1996): 232-249.

Rais, Rasul Bakhsh. "Afghanistan and the Regional Powers." *Asian Survey.* 33 (September 1993): 905-922.

Rashid, Ahmed. "Pakistan, Afghanistan and the Gulf." *MERIP Middle East Report.* (September-October 1987): 35-39.

Rashid, Jamal. "Pakistan and the Central Command." *MERIP Middle East Report.* 141 (July-August 1986): 28-34.

Reisman, W. Michael and James Silk. "Which Law Applies to the Afghan Conflict?" *American Journal of International Law.* 82 (July 1988): 459-486.

Robertson, William Glenn. "The Active Sanctuary: Challenge to Counterinsurgency." 19 May 1969. Unpublished paper in author's possession.

Rubinstein, Alvin Z. "The Soviet Union and Iran Under Khomeini." *International Affairs.* 57 (Autumn 1981): 599-617.

Salehyan, Idean. "No Shelter Here: Rebel Sanctuaries and International Conflict." Paper for the American Political Science Association Meeting. Washington, DC, 2005.

Shuffer, George M. "An Appropriate Response." *Military Review.* 49 (December 1969): 91-96.

Skidmore, David. "Carter and the Failure of Foreign Policy Reform." *Political Science Quarterly.* 108 (Winter 1993-1994): 399-729.

Sorley, Lewis. "Courage and Blood: South Vietnam's Repulse of the 1972 Easter Invasion." *Parameters.* 29 (Summer 1999): 38-56.

_____. "To Change a War: General Harold K. Johnson and the PROVN Study." *Parameters.* 28 (Spring 1998): 93-109.

Staniland, Paul. "Defeating Transnational Insurgencies: The Best Offense Is a Good Fence." *Washington Quarterly.* 29 (Winter 2005-06): 21-40.

Stork, Joe. "U.S. Involvement in Afghanistan." *MERIP Reports.* 89 (July-August 1980): 25-26.

Tarzi, Shah M. "Politics of the Afghan Resistance Movement." *Asian Survey.* 31 (June 1991): 479-495.

Thompson, Robert. "Squaring the Error." *Foreign Affairs.* 46 (April 1968): 442-453.

Turkoly-Joczik, Robert L. "Secrecy and Stealth: Cross-Border Reconnaissance in Indochina." *Military Intelligence Professional Bulletin.* 25 (July-September 1999): 47-52.

Valenta, Jiri. "From Prague to Kabul: The Soviet Style of Invasion." *International Security*. 5 (Autumn 1980): 114-141.

Vayrynen, Raimo. "Afghanistan." *Journal of Peace Research*. 17 (1980): 93-102.

Vertzberger, Yaacov. "Afghanistan in China's Policy." *Problems of Communism*. 31 (May-June 1982): 1-23.

Vien, Cao Van. "Vietnam: What Next?" *Military Review*. 52 (April 1972): 22-30.

Voorhies, David. "Stability Operations: The Legacy of Search and Attack." *Infantry*. 94 (May-June 2005): 27-34.

Weigley, Russell F. "The Soldier, the Statesman, and the Military Historian." *Journal of Military History*. 63 (October 1999): 807-822.

Weinbaum, Marvin G. "Pakistan and Afghanistan: The Strategic Relationship." *Asian Survey*. 31 (June 1991): 496-511.

Weiss, George. "Battle for Control of the Ho Chi Minh Trail." *Armed Forces Journal*. 108 (15 February 1971): 18-22.

Westad, Odd Arne. *"Concerning the Situation is 'A':* New Russian Evidence on the Soviet Intervention in Afghanistan." and "The Soviet Union and Afghanistan, 1978-1989." *Cold War International History Project Bulletin*, 8/9 (Winter 1996): 128-184.

Wriggins, W. Howard. "Pakistan's Search for a Foreign Policy After the Invasion of Afghanistan." *Pacific Affairs*. 57 (Summer 1984): 284-303.

Xiaoming Zhang. "The Vietnam War, 1964-1969: A Chinese Perspective." *Journal of Military History*. 60 (October 1996): 731-762.

Newspapers

Boston Globe.

Chicago Tribune.

Christian Science Monitor.

Los Angeles Times.

New York Times.

US Federal News Service.

Wall Street Journal.

Washington Post.

Theses and Dissertations

Banner, Gregory T. "The War for the Ho Chi Minh Trail." Master's Thesis. US Army Command and General Staff College, 1993.

Borer, Douglas Anthony. "Superpowers Defeated: A Comparison of Vietnam and Afghanistan." Ph.D. Dissertation. Boston University, 1993.

Hamilton, John R. "Defeating Insurgency on the Border." Marine Corps Command and Staff College, 1985. Online: www.globasecurity.org.

Higgins, James M. "The Misapplication of the Malayan Counterinsurgency Model to the Strategic Hamlet Program." Master's Thesis. US Army Command and General Staff College, 2001.

Macak, Richard J. "The CORDS Pacification Program: An Operational Level Campaign Plan in Low Intensity Conflict." SAMS Monograph. Fort Leavenworth, KS, May 1989.

Stevens, Richard L. "A History of the Ho Chi Minh Trail and the Role of Nature in the War in Viet Nam." Ph.D. Dissertation. University of Hawaii, 1990

About the Author

Prior to joining the Combat Studies Institute in December 2005, Thomas A. Bruscino, Jr. worked at the US Army Center of Military History in Washington, DC. Dr. Bruscino earned his B.A. in history from Adams State College in Alamosa, Colorado in 1999, his M.A. in American history from Ohio University in 2002, and his Ph.D. in American military history from Ohio University in 2005. His articles and review essays have appeared in the *Claremont Review of Books*, *Journal of America's Military Past*, *San Luis Valley Historian*, and *Reviews in American History*. Dr. Bruscino lives in Lansing, Kansas with his wife and two sons.

www.ingramcontent.com/pod-product-compliance
Lightning Source LLC
Chambersburg PA
CBHW070537290526
45790CB00002B/531